DISCOVERING
GOD'S WILL
FOR YOUR LIFE

WOMEN OF FAITH™
STUDY GUIDE SERIES

DISCOVERING GOD'S WILL FOR YOUR LIFE

FOREWORD BY

SHEILA WALSH

THOMAS NELSON PUBLISHERS
Nashville

The publishers are grateful to Christa Kinde for her collaboration,
writing skills, and editorial help in developing the content for this book.

Published by Thomas Nelson, Inc., P.O. Box 141000, Nashville, Tennessee, 37214.

ISBN 0-7852-4983-4

Printed in Canada.

03 04 05 06 07 – 5 4 3

✦ CONTENTS ✦

Discovering
God's Will
for Your Life

✦ FOREWORD ✦

As a teenager growing up in a small fishing town on the West coast of Scotland I had one question that followed me wherever I went. It popped up unexpectedly at picnics and outings, at school and in church, as I lay down to sleep at night and when I would wake on cold winter mornings savoring the last few moments before I had to get out of bed. It was a simple question but a weighty one, "What is God's will for my life?" My fear was that I would miss it. What if God was going to give me 'The Big Plan' at a Sunday evening service and I missed it because I stayed home to watch The Walton's Christmas special? Or what if I started well and then took a side turn and missed God's best plan? What if I married the wrong person or took the wrong job—would God by-pass my life? Would that mean that He didn't love me as much anymore? I was sure that my salvation was intact but I feared that I might miss the one thing that God had called me to and then He would give it to someone else. I imagined myself puttering through the rest of my life speculating as to where I went wrong and how life might have been different if I had just got it right.

My understanding has changed over the years. I know now that God loves to reveal His will to us. He is after our heart's allegiance, not our perfect performance. God is a loving Father not a circus side show vender hiding His plan for us under one of three coconut shells, camouflaging it by divine sleight of hand.

I am often asked at Women of Faith conferences:
How do I know what God's will is for my life?
How do I know who God wants me to marry?
How do I know what job to take?
If I miss God's will, have I ruined my life?

There are certain things that we know for sure. We know that it is God's will for us to love Him body, soul, mind, and heart and to love our neighbor as ourselves but what about the things we don't know for sure? The Bible doesn't tell us which car to buy or how many children we should have and at what age. This freedom can feel threatening at times but Jesus doesn't want us to live in fear. He said, "The thief comes only to steal and kill and destroy; I have come that they might have life, and have it to the full."—John 10:10.

Jesus talked about life, about living in liberty, and not being ruled by fear that we might make a wrong choice. Following God is a great adventure. Jesus is with us, always. We have not been left in the dark. There is a pathway. Welcome to the adventure!

— Sheila Walsh

✦ INTRODUCTION ✦

There are times when oh, what we wouldn't give for a little direction. Desperately we long for God's guidance. How many times have I heard people say, "I really want to do what God wants me to do, but what is it? What is His will anyway?"

Luci Swindoll

There are so many big decisions in life! Should I get married? Should we start a family? Should I stay home with my children? Should I go back to school? Should we look for a new church? Should we move? Should the kids go to a private school? Should I look for a new job? In the major choices we face throughout our lifetimes, we want so badly to do the right thing. We want to follow God's plan for our lives. We want to do God's will.

Then there are all the little decisions in life! Do I have time to join a Bible study? Should we buy a puppy? Will the car make it another year? Can we afford to give extra money for missions? Should I introduce myself to the new neighbors? Will I get tired of this wallpaper in three months? What should I make for dinner? In the little decisions of our everyday lives, does God have a plan for us, too?

Well, the Bible's lessons for us are not quite so specific. We cannot turn the pages of Scripture and discover that according to 3 Hesitations 21:4 that Bernice should be a veterinarian when she grows up. However, there are verses that actually say "This is the will of God."

"Teach me to do Your will, for You are my God.
May Your gracious Spirit
lead me forward on a firm footing."

Psalm 143:10, NLT

CHAPTER 1

WHERE THERE'S A WILL...

"YOUR WILL BE DONE ON EARTH
AS IT IS IN HEAVEN."

Matthew 6:10, NKJV

s we ponder the big questions in life, our minds wander down well-worn paths. "Who am I?" "What should I do?" "Where should I go?" "Why am I here?" We long to do something of value, to be recognized, to distinguish ourselves, and to leave a legacy. As Christians, we also wish to discover God's will for our lives. Surely He is already laying the groundwork for our lofty aspirations in life. Then, when things don't quite meet our expectations, we are perturbed. And if they take a dire turn into disaster, we are perplexed. What went wrong? We missed the point.

The thing is, God's will is just that—*God's* will. He tends to do things His way, in His time, according to His own plan, and with His own purposes in mind. God often ignores our agenda! Over and over the Scriptures bring up an important theme: "My ways are not like your ways!" Sometimes we need a gentle reminder that He's not like us.

CLEARING ✦ THE ✦ COBWEBS

Consider these two words: *willfulness* and *willingness*. Just a few letters are different, but the meaning is altered considerably. How would you compare these two attitudes?

1. Have you ever tried to reason with a two-year-old? A mother can begin calmly enough, but when faced with the one-track-minded, stubborn resolve of a selfish little person, she is reduced to begging, bribing, threatening, shouting, compromise, and even surrender. How are we like a self-absorbed toddler compared to God?

> *The wonder of it all is that the Lord can use everything for whatever purposes He chooses. Not to mention everyone.*
>
> Patsy Clairmont

2. Consider Isaiah 55:8. "'My thoughts are not your thoughts, Nor are your ways My ways,' says the Lord." How does our limited perspective affect our day-to-day living?

*S*ometimes we find ourselves in a clash of wills. God's way just isn't what we had in mind. In the midst of troubling circumstances, God does not despise us for our honest questions. He welcomes us to pour out our troubled hearts before His throne. In fact, when our pain is so deep, His Spirit even provides groanings on our behalf.

More than one of God's chosen prophets has stood before Him and cried out "Why?" However, at the end of each rant, God gently reminds the mere human of the way things are. Some of us might need to be nudged back into our place once in a while as well.

"So you see, God shows mercy to some just because He wants to, and He chooses to make some people refuse to listen. Well then, you might say, 'Why does God blame people for not listening? Haven't they simply done what He made them to do?' No, don't say that. Who are you, a mere human being, to criticize God?

Should the thing that was created say to the one who made it, 'Why have you made me like this?' When a potter makes jars out of clay, doesn't he have a right to use the same lump of clay to make one jar for decoration and another to throw garbage into? God has every right to exercise His judgment and His power, but He also has the right to be very patient with those who are the objects of His judgment and are fit only for destruction. He also has the right to pour out the riches of His glory upon those He prepared to be the objects of His mercy."
—Romans 9:18–23, NLT

3. Read Romans 9:18–23 above. Do you ever feel like the pot that says "Why have you made me like this?" Would you love to ask God, "Why?" about some aspect of your life?

4. Something within us fights against being told what to do. We are constantly urged to fight for our rights, to value individuality, to find our own path, to sport our own unique style. According to Romans 9, what are God's rights? What are ours?

> *"People on earth are not truly important. God does what He wants with the powers of heaven and the people on earth. No one can stop His powerful hand or question what He does."*
>
> Daniel 4:35, NCV

5. Make no mistake, though He has His own motives, God *is* at work in our lives. Philippians 2:13 reminds us that "it is God who works in you." But the verse goes on to say *why* He is working: "both to will and to do for His good pleasure." What does Paul mean "to will and to do"?

> *"When God says His purpose will stand and that He does what He pleases, my part in it all is to sit back humbly, receive whatever it is He plans for me, and believe in what I see."*
>
> Marilyn Meberg

6. Look up Romans 12:2. How does Paul define God's will here?

So, we are insignificant. Compared to God we are nothing. We are blades of grass. We are specks. We are nothing but dust (Ps. 103:14). Perhaps we have overestimated our own value? How very . . . encouraging?

But wait! God does not always humble us. Often the Scriptures remind us that we are precious in His sight. Though we are very small, we have been created to glorify God in our lives.

7. Remember the song "Jesus Loves the Little Children"? That last line states: "red and yellow, black and white, they are precious in His sight." God has a plan and a place for each of His precious daughters. Read John 6:39. What does Jesus say is His Father's will?

> *I am not an afterthought. All God's love-inspired preplanning for each of us is not haphazard or impersonal. His timing may throw me or His sovereign plan may grieve me, but I am always sheltered in His sovereign hand. Can I rest in that? Can I quit resisting that? Not always, but that's my humanness interfering with my acceptance of His divineness.*
>
> Marilyn Meberg

✦ DIGGING DEEPER ✦

Look up Psalm 95:10 and Hebrews 3:10. The writer of Hebrews is quoting from the Psalms passage, and speaks of people who do not know God's ways. Contrast that with the beautiful description in Isaiah 58:2, with a people who delight to know God's ways!

✦ PONDER & PRAY ✦

This week, pray that God will open your eyes to see the people and things around you the way that He sees them! Allow Him to help you distinguish between the things that are fleeting in this life (like television sitcoms, manicured nails, and immaculate homes) and the things that will last into eternity (like God, His Word, and people). Ask Him to shape your life so that He can use you for His glory.

✦ TRINKETS TO TREASURE ✦

At the close of every Women of Faith conference, women are asked to play a little game of pretend. Each conference guest is asked to imagine that a gift has been placed in their hands—one from each of the speakers. These gifts serve as reminders of the different lessons shared by the Women of Faith. This study guide will carry on this tradition! At the close of each lesson, you will be presented with a small gift. Though imaginary, it will serve to remind you of the things you have learned. Think of it as a souvenir! Souvenirs are little trinkets we pick up on our journeys to remind us of where we have been. They keep us from forgetting the path we have traveled. Hide these little treasures in your heart, for as you ponder on them, they will draw you closer to God!

✦ TRINKETS TO TREASURE ✦

Our token gift for this week is a tiny clay pot, to remind us of our smallness and fragility compared to our great God. Though a humble pot is made from mud, it has been shaped in such a way to make it useful. Remember that no matter how shapeless your pot may seem, God has chosen to pour out His riches and glory into it.

✦ NOTES & PRAYER REQUESTS ✦

CHAPTER 2

GOD'S WILL IS RELATIONSHIP

"WHOEVER DOES THE WILL OF GOD IS MY BROTHER AND MY SISTER AND MOTHER."

Mark 3:35

Have you ever had to fill out a form? You know the kind: name, birth date, and social security number. Then there comes a line that is always cause for pause. "What is your religious affiliation?" With furrowed eyebrows, I think back and consider my options. Some of my first memories are of long wooden pews and stained glass windows. Then my parents enthusiastically switched to a completely different church where hands were raised and worship was rather rowdy. Then, as a preteen, I was sent to a conservative school where boys' hairlines and girls' hemlines were strictly monitored. If Christians were given pedigrees, I would be considered a mutt!

So how do we fill in the blank? Do the makers of these lists really want that much information? Do they care? So do we declare a denominational preference? With a sigh, I carefully print the word *Christian* on the form.

CLEARING ✦ THE ✦ COBWEBS

What relationships in your life have most shaped your Christian walk? What did these people help you to see?

The makers of such lists simply categorize us as an adherent to one of the many different religions out there. They have no idea what that single word entails. We are not just Christians, as opposed to people of other religious groups. We are Christians—chosen, forgiven, redeemed, saved, changed, filled, sealed, adopted, and thankful! To them, it is the answer to a fill-in-the-blank question. To us, it is everything! Christianity is not just a religion—it is a relationship.

1. God has promised to fill in the blanks in our relationships. He is a parent to the orphan, a husband to the widow, a friend to the lonely, a brother to the believer. Doing God's will secures our relationship with God. How has God met your need for Him?

If I could say only one thing, it would be simple and to the point: God knows all about you. He knows your good days and your bad days. He knows the noble thoughts and the shameful thoughts. He sees your devotion and your indifference. And He loves you— totally, completely, passionately, boundlessly. Forever.

Sheila Walsh

2. Look up Mark 3:35. What kind of relationship results from doing the will of God?

3. So, you are a believer and you have a relationship with God. Great! The next logical question seems to be "So what do I *do* now?" The answer is surprising! John 6:29 says, "The work God wants you to do is this: Believe the One He sent." God wants believers to *believe* Him. What does that mean?

4. If we really take God seriously and take Jesus at His Word, how should our beliefs affect our everyday lives? Have you allowed what you believe to transform you?

> *Getting into heaven isn't dependent on our doing anything correctly, praise God! Redemption rests on the finished work of Christ on the Cross. When Jesus died, He did so for you and me and our deceitful hearts that can never get it right.*
>
> Luci Swindoll

*S*ometimes a parent can look into the face of their child and they are struck to the very core of their being with love. The emotion is so intense that it almost hurts, and often that sweet sting brings tears to the eyes. Mother-love must be one of the strongest feelings possible. It can cause moms to do the strangest things!

Yet God loves us *more* than that. "In His goodness He chose to make us His own children by giving us His true Word. And we, out of all creation, became His choice possession" (James 1:18, NLT). He did some pretty wild things on our behalf, too! How astonishing to find the Master of the Universe taking time to build relationships with friends and disciples. "No longer do I call you servants . . . but I have called you friends" (Matt. 15:15, NKJV). That hand of friendship has been extended to us as well!

5. Look up 1 Timothy 2:4. This is a pretty clear statement of what God wants. What does Paul say here?

6. In fact, God is so anxious for our salvation, that He is allowing time to pass so that more and more of us can become Christians. According to Matthew 18:14, what does Jesus say is *not* God's will?

7. Don't you get frustrated with people who can't seem to read a clock? The kids dilly-dally around when their rooms need tidying. Our less-than-punctual friends can't seem to remember what time we agreed to meet at the park. Peter faced people who were criticizing God for being too slow. Look up 2 Peter 3:9. Is this a case of pokey-ness? Who can you think of that can still benefit from God's delay?

As a Christian, the Spirit is drawing you in God's direction. There is a longing for His Word, for prayer. Those are the building blocks of a relationship—and a divine one at that! Though you cannot see this new Father, this new Brother, this new Friend, there is no doubt about His presence. He has chosen you, and welcomes you to know Him better. God assures us He has a plan for our lives—a purpose in our place here.

Though His purposes may only become clear to you in hindsight, you can walk forward in confidence. He who has led you safely thus far will surely lead you on!

8. Many women have taken Jeremiah 29:11 as their life's verse. Look it up! Why do God's words here bring us such comfort and confidence?

> *There is no guarantee that if we had done a part of our lives differently things would end up any different. We have to trust the God of the universe who directs the outcome of all things that He will do that which ultimately needs to be done (in spite of us if necessary).*
>
> Patsy Clairmont

9. What is another aspect of God's will as found in 1 Corinthians 1:1?

10. Calling does not always entail full-time Christian ministry. Some women are called to be wives and mothers. Others are called to be friends, helpers, encouragers, intercessors, listeners, teachers, advisors, protectors, leaders, and motivators. Do you feel a calling of God for your life? What niche have you found in this season of life?

✦ Digging Deeper ✦

How do you build a relationship with someone you cannot see? People are trying it all the time nowadays on the Internet! But we are talking about God here, and He doesn't seem to have an email address. Though our pursuit of God might seem one-sided at times, let's look at some passages that assure us God is find-able and know-able.

- Deuteronomy 4:29
- Proverbs 8:17
- Jeremiah 29:13
- Matthew 7:7
- Acts 17:27

✦ Ponder & Pray ✦

This week find ways to deepen your relationship with God. Choose a passage of Scripture to read and reread. Memorize one of the verses from the Digging Deeper section. Go for a prayer walk and tell Him about your day. Tack up a hymn to sing while you do the dishes. Start journaling your prayers. Type Him an email! Pray that God would reward your earnest seeking by revealing Himself to you.

✦ Trinkets to Treasure ✦

This week's token is a reminder that we have a relationship, not just a religion. We hear of friendship rings and promise rings, engagement rings, wedding rings, and anniversary rings. The bands on our fingers become physical reminders of the relationships we hold dear. Your trinket for this week is a pretty little ring to remind you of your pledge to One who loves you more deeply than words can express. Slip it onto your finger every time you mull over Jesus' Word, and allow what you believe in your heart to transform your life.

✦ Notes & Prayer Requests ✦

CHAPTER 3

Is God's Will So Mysterious?

The people asked Jesus,
"What are the things God wants us to do?"

John 6:28, NCV

How can I know God's will for my life?" "Am I outside of God's will in this?" "What is God's will for us?" "If God wills it, we will proceed." "I am praying that God will show us His will." "I want to be in God's perfect will for my life!"

Why does "God's will" seem to be such an elusive thing? God's ways may be unsearchable, but is His will unknowable? Some days we are never quite sure if we are on the right track.

So, how do we find God's will for our life? Many of us have looked for a magic formula to determine the will of God. Some of us have tried the strangest things in order to figure it out! Moments of struggle have found us in some quiet corner, allowing our Bible to drop open, and with closed eyes pointing out a verse on the page. Desperate times have driven us to make strange bargains. "Lord, if this is your will for my life, then please let the next car that drives past my

Clearing ✦ the ✦ Cobwebs

If you were forced to simplify your life down to the very basics of survival, what few precious items would you keep with you? What non-essential items would be hardest to give up?

house be a red one!" We look for a verse. We pray for a sign. We wish for an arrow painted across the sky.

Thankfully, we do not need to abandon common sense in seeking God's leading! Let's get down to brass tacks then. What are the steps for finding God's will when we are faced with a difficult decision?

1. The first place to turn is God's own Word. Luci Swindoll says, "The Bible is very definitive about the responsibility of a disciple of Christ." How can we look to the Bible for decision-making advice *now* when it was written centuries and even millennia ago?

> *I've never understood nor trusted people who say "I woke up this morning and my wife was cooking bacon. I knew that I was supposed to go to Israel." I think God has more straightforward ways to lead His children.*
>
> Luci Swindoll

2. We are seeking God's will, but the only way we can please Him is if we know what He wants! Romans 2:18 says: "You know what He wants you to do and what is important, because you have learned the law" (NCV). Then Jesus came with a whole new way of doing things. Look at John 15, especially verses 8–12. What are some of the things asked of us here?

3. So, is God's Word really just a guidebook for living?

4. The next clue we have in searching out God's will is our circumstances. Do you have a story of a time when God's hand was clear in closing one door in your life and opening another door in an unexpected way?

*O*ur family was growing out of our little two-bedroom home. It was time to look for something a bit bigger. A "For Sale" sign went up on a beautiful place near our church. It was a vast place and seemed to fit our needs perfectly. We breathed a prayer for God to open or close the doors ahead of us. Then, with barely contained excitement, we made an offer and sat back to see what might happen.

Though our realtor checked in with us on a weekly basis, one delay followed another. Since we were in no hurry, we assured the realtor that we could wait for the seller to straighten out his affairs. Months passed, and we started boxing up some of our stuff just in case the deal should go through. Christmas neared, and we debated whether or not to put up the tree, just in case the deal should go through. Friends were on standby to help us move, just in case the deal should go through.

Then, my husband got a call. There was a job opportunity within his company. It would mean a promotion. It would mean a larger salary. It would mean less time on the road and more time with the family. And, it would mean moving out of state. Suddenly, the door slammed shut on the "ideal" house. We loaded our already-packed boxes and headed for the open door of an entirely different home hundreds of miles away.

> *"If we're not intimately familiar with His manual [the Bible], what are the chances we'll understand His ways?"*
>
> Patsy Clairmont

Though the delays in our life may seem frustrating, it is good to remember that only God knows what is around the next bend!

5. The third thing to seek out when trying to discern God's will is wise counsel. Who do you turn to for advice when facing a decision?

6. The Bible never tells us to go it alone. Solomon gives wise counsel in his many proverbs. His advice is to get good advice! "Those who take advice are wise" (Prov. 13:10, NCV). What does Proverbs 12:5 say about people who always think they are right?

*A*re all decisions big decisions? No! It is often the little decisions in life that are the hardest to handle. Life is full of everyday choices.

Should I take the time to fix supper, or can I just run through the drive-through again? Should I eat another cookie, or stop? Should I splurge on a new outfit, or save the money for a real need? Should I wash the dishes now, or take the time to read to my son? Should I commit myself to helping organize that event at church, or leave my schedule free for my family's sake? Should I stay up late and watch a movie when I know I'll regret it tomorrow morning? Should I take care of it now, or add it to my growing to-do list?

Can we apply the same principles for making the big decisions in life to our little daily choices? You bet! The Spirit's promptings are there just the same. We know right from wrong—it's been part of our wiring since the

> *If God's Word, your circumstances, and the counsel of others line up, and if you sense His provision, I'd say go for it. And don't be surprised if, in some peculiar way, God confirms the call.*
>
> Luci Swindoll

Fall (Gen. 2:17; 3:7). And though many of our little choices do not necessarily lead us into sin, we know in our hearts when we have not chosen the wiser path.

7. Check out the first half of Galatians 3:19. What is one of the purposes of the Bible, or "the law" as stated there?

8. Read Romans 7:15–19. We can all identify with Paul's struggle here. Even when we know in our heart of hearts what we should do, it is still a struggle at times to choose to do the right thing. Why is it so hard to say "no" to ourselves?

> *My experience with the prompting of the Holy Spirit has been that when He does, there is an indescribable peace within your body, mind, and spirit that you feel but can't explain to anyone who hasn't experienced it. And of course, God's Spirit would never direct us to do anything contrary to Scripture, so we have a guidebook that can help us. You've probably said in your heart in certain situations, "I knew in my heart that such and such was . . ." or "I had a feeling that . . ." Those are probably times that God's Spirit is prompting you.*
>
> Thelma Wells

9. So, is it hopeless? Are we stuck in our sinning state? Look up Romans 6:6–7. Does this promise bring encouragement to your heart? How will this truth change you from now on?

✦ DIGGING DEEPER ✦

We hear people talk about God opening and closing doors all the time. It's part of our Christian jargon. But did you know that the phrase "open door" is really biblical? Look up the following verses, and see how Paul speaks of God's working in his ministry.

- Acts 14:27
- 1 Corinthians 16:9
- 2 Corinthians 2:12
- Colossians 4:3

✦ PONDER & PRAY ✦

When those big decisions in life come, you know just how to handle them now. This week pray that God would help you to slow down and recognize the little decisions built into your days. Let Him show you the choices you are making, and test them against His Word and His will. Draw courage from the knowledge that your sinful self has no power over your saved self! Allow this time of self-examination to draw you even closer to His side.

✦ TRINKETS TO TREASURE ✦

Your gift this week is a tiny golden arrow, small enough to hold in the palm of your hand. Like the arrows we wish God would paint across the sky for us, it will remind you of the direction you should be going. Following His Word, circumstances, and wise counsel, you can pursue His will with confidence. The size of your wee trinket also serves as a reminder. The decisions you face are rarely big ones. In the smallest choices of your daily life, let your arrow remind you God can be glorified here as well.

✦ Notes & Prayer Requests ✦

CHAPTER 4

WAR OF THE WILLS

"HE NO LONGER SHOULD LIVE THE REST OF HIS TIME IN THE FLESH FOR THE LUSTS OF MEN, BUT FOR THE WILL OF GOD."

1 Peter 4:2, NKJV

Some days I am the queen of rationalization! When temptation is lurking, I have these small chats with myself. These little talks are necessary to lull my conscience to sleep!

I am persuasive. I am smooth. I'm so convincing, I have often wondered if my talents would be put to better use in some marketing firm. After all, these are the wizards who have convinced us of all sorts of outrageous things. With honed skill and honeyed words, the world tells us that we should follow our fancy. If it looks good, tastes good, sounds good, or feels good, then we need it. Never mind if it is *actually* good for us!

According to these master salesmen, we need to awaken our senses (Nescafe®). That way we'll know that life tastes good (Coca Cola®). Of course we deserve a break today (McDonalds®). Then, we should obey our thirst (Sprite®). Why? Because I'm worth it (L'oreal®). After all, you know you want to (Pringles®). So, just do it (Nike®)!

CLEARING ✦ THE ✦ COBWEBS

The old joke was that when a woman was depressed, all she needed was a new hat to cheer her up. When you are feeling a little low, what are the kinds of things that really turn your day around? What little things help you swing your mood back into the "good" zone?

But the Bible reminds us that we *used* to live to fulfill the desires of our hearts and minds (Eph. 2:3), but no more! Now we need to place our will in subjection to God's will. Unfortunately, the world around us provides a big cheering section for self and selfish desires. It's hard to ignore the fast talk and flattery. Our choices are very important, though, because in the battle between our will and God's will, we get to decide who wins!

1. In order to follow God's will, we are confronted with a natural impulse to make selfish choices. What are some of the urges that come easily to our bent towards sin? Look in Galatians 5:19–21 for a comprehensive list.

> *"Let the words of my mouth and the meditation of my heart be acceptable in Your sight, O Lord, my strength and my Redeemer."*
>
> Psalm 19:14, NKJV

2. Nasty list! But let's take a look at the flipside! Galatians 5:22–23 gives us a list of the works of the Spirit. What are the nine characteristics of our lives when we are pursuing God's will?

3. God asks us to bypass what comes naturally. Christians are to be a "peculiar people" (1 Pet. 2:9, KJV), acting and reacting differently than the rest of the people in the world. Have you gone beyond the call of courtesy? Has your attitude startled someone lately?

4. Jesus leads the way in selflessness. Look at John 6:38 for His words on the matter. What was Jesus' incentive for setting aside His rights in that way? What would it take for *you* to follow His example?

> *Christ longs for us to experience radical transformation of what comes naturally. Isn't that outlandish? All I can say is that it's a good thing our God is big because, if we're going to be that different from our human nature, He's going to be very busy. Talk about a full-time job!*
>
> Patsy Clairmont

5. Peter makes it pretty clear we *are* expected to follow Christ's example. Look up 1 Peter 4:2. What does Peter say we should live for?

ewly mobile in a six-wheeled "bouncer coupe," my son began to explore the exciting world that had now come into reach. His walker-bound status forced us to rethink our previous attempts at baby-proofing our home. As I firmly but gently removed my baby's hand from the dirt of another houseplant, he turned his eyes to me, pushed out his little lower lip, and burst into angry tears.

> *Belonging to Jesus means you've been given a heart transplant. With a new heart, He gives the power to be joyful, exuberant, and thankful. Eternal values replace temporary ones.*
>
> Barbara Johnson

Astonished, I rocked back on my heels to watch his first tantrum. Where did he learn this? He was only nine months old! I sighed at the undeniable fact my little angel was a little sinner after all.

We start early, don't we? Sin holds the human race in a stranglehold of selfishness. Paul puts it this way: "you were slaves of sin" (Rom. 6:17, 20).

6. So how do we turn the corner, and change from slavery to sin to serving the Savior? Time to turn to Romans 12:2.

7. Is this a one-time transformation or a long process?

> *Decide to accept the path God has given you with courage, grace, and humor. Don't deny reality, but choose to think on what is excellent and praiseworthy.*
>
> Luci Swindoll

8. How do we go about "renewing" our minds? Find Paul's suggestions in Philippians 4:8. What things in your life fit these criteria? Is there anything in your life filling your mind with something *other* than these things?

9. Are we responsible for our own transformation? What does God reveal to us in Ephesians 2:8–10?

✦ DIGGING DEEPER ✦

The dictionary defines *delight* as "giving great pleasure or joy." When we pursue the Lord and find delight in His ways, we are changed women. He shapes our hearts and makes us desire Him even more. In Psalm 37:4, David says "Delight yourself in the Lord, and He shall give you the desires of your heart." This is *not* a promise to give you whatever you want. Instead, it is a promise the Lord will transform what you desire! We will hunger and thirst after righteousness (Matt. 5:6)! Let's look at some more verses which speak about the transformation and delights of our heart.

- Psalm 1:2
- Psalm 51:10
- Job 33:26
- Romans 7:22
- Psalm 21:2
- Psalm 94:19
- Isaiah 11:3
- Psalm 40:8
- Proverbs 11:20
- Isaiah 58:2

✦ PONDER & PRAY ✦

Take this week's lesson to heart, and pray that God will help you to see where His hand has been at work in your life. Can you look back and see changes within your Spirit over the years since you were saved? Lift up songs of praise to God for His workmanship! With that encouragement held close, look at the day which stands before you. Pray that God will continue to shape you into a godly woman. Pray that He will indeed give you the desires of your heart.

✦ TRINKETS TO TREASURE ✦

This week's little gift will help you remember your mind is in the process of being renewed. It is a tiny garbage can! Set the little trash bin where it will catch your eye. The first words to leap to your mind are "Garbage in; garbage out." Then, you can bring to mind those precious verses from Philippians 4:8: "whatever things are true, whatever things are noble, whatever things are just, whatever things are pure, whatever things are lovely, whatever things are of good report, if there is any virtue and if there is anything praiseworthy—meditate on these things" (NKJV). You are precious to God, and He is transforming your life into something truly beautiful. As you chase after Him in pursuing His will, fill your life with things lovely and true!

✦ NOTES & PRAYER REQUESTS ✦

CHAPTER 5

WHAT ARE YOU CHASING?

"What does the Lord your God require of you?
He requires you to fear Him, to live according
to His will, to love and worship Him with
all your heart and soul."

Deuteronomy 10:12, NLT

Have you ever met somebody who has a hobby? Not a simple, cross-stitch-during-the-evening-news kind of a hobby, but a my-life-revolves-around-this kind of a hobby.

For example, some people love barbershop quartet singing. They belong to their local chapter, and they have formed their own quartet. They plan their vacations around district competitions and a couple weekends a year are devoted to special music camps. They have barbershop cassette tapes in their cars. They have barbershop quartet videos next to their television sets. They subscribe to their own magazine—the *Harmonizer*. They own ties with musical notes and lapel pins with red and white striped barbershop poles on them. They wear straw hats and sport handlebar moustaches. Their belts have special leather pouches, where they keep the pitch pipes. They can spend hours discussing the presence (or lack) of a

CLEARING ✦ THE ✦ COBWEBS

An old proverb says that "the main thing is to keep the main thing the main thing." That's harder to do than we might think. In today's busy society, if you're just *maintaining*, you're actually ahead of most folks! Do you have a "main thing" around which you plan your days?

"circle of fifths" in a show tune, and the cost of bringing in professional choreographers to polish up their choruses' routine before the big competition. They have their own society, official website, and even a hall of fame (It's in Kenosha, Wisconsin). Valentine's Day is spent going around delivering singing valentines to blushing recipients. They know all the oldies by heart, like "My Wild Irish Rose," "Let Me Call You Sweetheart" and "Heart of My Heart." For those who love the old barbershop style, singing the good old songs has become their way of life!

1. Do you have a hobby which influences your everyday actions and decisions? Are you an obsessive crafter, quilter, collector, clowner, shopper, singer, surfer, scrapbooker, hiker, biker, raiser, rider, racer, reader, gardener, or gourmet?

If I had the opportunity, I would get up every morning and speak somewhere. That's my passion in life. God called me to do that and continually gives me everything it takes to speak—the knowledge, the engagements, and the words to say. I love it so much that I give away a lot of time, effort, energy, and experience doing what I'm called to do without getting overly tired.

Thelma Wells

2. Peter says now we should "be anxious to do the will of God" (1 Pet. 4:2, NLT). This implies some excitement, some gusto, some eagerness. How would you describe the stirrings in your own heart on God's behalf?

3. How are you supposed to be doing the will of God? Check out Ephesians 6:6 for the proper manner!

4. What kinds of things do you like to do so well, you look forward to them with anticipation, then throw yourself into them with abandon once it's time to begin? Okay, how about the flipside. What tasks do you absolutely dread, and the whole process is a drudgery for you?

5. How does Paul encourage us to face our daily tasks? Look up Colossians 3:23. Does this perspective change *your* perspective?

*W*hat are you chasing? What captures your imagination? Where do you spend your spare moments? What draws your attention? What do you daydream about? What events do you center your day around? Where do your extra pennies go? What tunes run through your mind? What is your first thought when you wake up in the morning?

Many of the things which hold our time and attention are really just good clean fun. No harm in that! God has made us creative creatures, and we take great pleasure and satisfaction in pursuing our various interests.

Priorities are important to keep in check.

So what's the difference? Why do I sometimes get bogged down with chores, hating the day? Then, at other times, I get fired up with enthusiasm, loving the day? Perspective! Perspective is everything. Paul encourages us to do whatever we do with all our hearts. He tells us to pour our soul into it. The busiest days can become our most joyful.

Luci Swindoll

I decided that I wanted to do something to add meaning to all the boring routines in my day. I decided to celebrate them, to make them stand out as worthwhile accomplishments. Each time I faced a tedious, mundane task, I imbued it with enthusiasm. I tried to think up some personally edifying reason for doing what I was doing. No trivial task was overlooked. I wanted to fill each one with a sense of being golden.

Barbara Johnson

When a hobby begins to nibble away at the time and attention which belong to God, our relationship with Him begins to slide quickly.

Give God the priority! Make room for Him in your day. Let Him capture your attention, draw your heart, and run tunes of praise through your mind.

6. Even back in the days of Moses, God's will was the same. What does Deuteronomy 10:12 urge the followers of God to do?

> *I've always believed that those who want to know God's will can know it. It's His responsibility to reveal it.*
>
> Luci Swindoll

7. Like a dog, chasing our own tails, we rush through our days trying to hold our schedule together. We really are busy! But what are we pursuing? Turn to Matthew 6:33. What does Jesus say that we should want most?

8. Let's look at another verse where Jesus talks about wholehearted pursuit— Mark 12:30. We are commanded to give our all in what areas?

9. What does "with all your heart" mean? How about "with all your mind"? And how can you pursue the will of God "with all your strength"?

✦ DIGGING DEEPER ✦

The game is afoot! The thrill of the chase! Cover your eyes and count to ten! Sometimes our Christian walk is like playing a game of hide-and-seek. At times, God seems to be hiding from us, and we must earnestly seek Him before He shows Himself. Then, it's our turn to hide, and like Jonah we fool ourselves into believing that we can elude His loving gaze. We've already studied the verses that assure us when we look for Him, God can be found. Let's explore a few verses that mention God's search for us!

- 1 Samuel 13:14
- Psalm 119:176
- Isaiah 62:12
- Ezekiel 34:12
- Luke 15:8–10
- Matthew 18:11–14
- Luke 19:10

✦ PONDER & PRAY ✦

Pray for the Lord to renew your love for Him, and to give you a fresh excitement for His ways! May the Spirit of the Lord stir up your heart with an eagerness for the things of the Lord. Let Him draw you into His Word and towards meaningful conversations in prayer. Then, when faced with everyday tasks, look for ways to give them meaning. Send up prayers for the owners of each item of clothing you fold. Give praise for the plenty of food on the table as you clean up the dishes that fill the sink. Do some soul-searching in the shower, so your heart comes away as clean as your body. Find little ways to invite the Lord more and more into your day!

✦ TRINKETS TO TREASURE ✦

This week's trinket will bring back the verse in Ephesians 6:6: "Do the will of God with all your heart" (NLT). Of course it is a heart—one for your refrigerator! Don't follow the Savior's call in a half-hearted way. Give Him your all! Just like the refrigerator magnet clings to the kitchen fridge, let your heart be drawn to God!

✦ NOTES & PRAYER REQUESTS ✦

_____

_____

_____

_____

_____

_____

_____

_____

_____

_____

CHAPTER 6

PLANNING FOR GOD'S WILL

YOU OUGHT TO SAY "IF THE LORD WILLS, WE SHALL LIVE AND DO THIS OR THAT."

James 4:15, NKJV

on't you just love it when the in-laws come for a long-anticipated visit? Or how about hosting your whole Sunday school class for a cook-out? Ever made plans for your daughter's graduation open house? The date is set, the calendar is marked, and we start to make preparations. With company coming, we suddenly look around our house and see it through new eyes—through *their* eyes. Oh dear! That room needs painting, those shelves need dusting, this closet needs cleaning out. What *is* that stuck on the ceiling? Suddenly, we feel the urge to re-wallpaper, wash curtains, and iron pillowcases. You'd think Martha Stewart was coming over for inspection! The far corners of the bathroom get a good scrubbing, and we wash the drips and smudges off the fronts of our kitchen cupboards. It's all stuff we've been meaning to do. Having company just kind of helped move things along!

CLEARING ✦ THE ✦ COBWEBS

Is there something in your house right now that you would absolutely have to change, move, fix, or clean before you would invite company over? How long would it take to do it?

Have you ever awakened one morning and the thought popped into your head "Maybe today Jesus will come back?" His Coming has been long-anticipated, but we're not quite sure what His travel plans are. He could drop in any time. Does this thought make you look around with new eyes? Have you ever been given the spiritual insight that comes with looking at life with God's eyes? Are there things you have been living with you would hate for Him to come in and see? Have you been putting off some of the things you know you should be doing on a daily basis?

When we start planning for God's will in our days, we experience change in perspective!

1. Are you a planner? Do you enjoy planning things almost more than actually doing them? Or are you the spontaneous type, and love the freedom to change your schedule all around on a whim? Okay. So how is God able to use your particular style?

2. What are some of the benefits in planning ahead? Can we plan for God's will?

Live every day to fulfill your personal mission. God has a reason for whatever season you are living through right now. A season of loss or blessing? A season of activity or hibernation? A season of growth or incubation? You may think you're on a detour, but God knows the best way for you to reach your destination.

Barbara Johnson

3. We know that we should be looking to God for His guidance in our decisions. After all, He has made plans! What does Jeremiah 29:11 say about God's agenda?

4. Some New Testament Christians once tried to talk Paul out of some travel plans. They felt he was putting himself into unnecessary danger, but Paul was insistent. He stuck to his plan. Look in Acts 21:14—What was their reaction?

When I was a child, I learned a few common abbreviations that floated around in Christian circles. PTL meant "praise the Lord" and TLC meant "tender loving care." They were cute shortcuts, and seemed to catch on. In school, girls would sign their notes BFF for "best friends forever" or they would borrow Tigger's TTFN, meaning "ta ta for now." In these days of email and chat rooms, abbreviations are more and more commonplace. LOL means "laugh out loud" and BRB means "be right back."

Long enough ago that many of us have forgotten, Christians used a similar abbreviation in their handwritten letters—D.V. These two letters stand for the Latin words Deo Volente (pronounced DAY-o vo-LEN-tay), which basically means "God willing." Holiday plans, promised visits, and travel arrangements would all be followed by the two little letters, D.V. It was a way of reminding each other that our lives are in God's hands, and our paths must follow God's will. It is a quaint little tradition. Why not revive it in your next letter!

> *What gets in the way of my ability to live in the moment is trying to do too many things at once. I can't possibly finish it all, and I don't get anything done! The most wonderful truth behind dealing with all our distractions is that we don't need to organize and plan with our natural ability alone. The Holy Spirit gives us everything we need. If we yield ourselves to Him, He will order our steps according to His purposes.*
>
> Thelma Wells

5. Many Christians have a little phrase that they drop into their conversations now and then. When they speak of their plans, they say "Lord willing, I will see you next week." Or they will say "Should the Lord tarry, we will see these future plans come to pass." This might seem a bit quirky, but it is based on Scripture. What does Paul say in Romans 1:10?

> *Every good life is a balance of duty and bliss. We will be called upon to do things we would rather not. Sometimes people say "Just follow your heart," but it isn't necessarily the right approach. We have to weigh decisions by mind and spirit and by the Word of God.*
>
> Barbara Johnson

6. Now take a look at James 4:13–15. What does James urge Christians to say? And why?

7. Have you been making plans lately? Have you asked God to let you see them through His eyes? How would a change in your perspective affect your planning process?

8. How much planning goes into your life? Do you have a steady routine? Do you always serve meatloaf on Monday nights? Do you meet your coworkers for lunch every Friday? Do you always pop popcorn before bedtime? What are your everyday traditions?

When I was a child, I loved coming down the stairs and into the kitchen to find my mother busy at the counter. Golden Tupperware canisters of flour and sugar were brought down. The little crank nut-grinder was filled with walnuts. And the unmistakable smells of cinnamon and nutmeg met my upturned nose. "What are you making?" Then would come the answer that sunk all hopes, "Something for church." Oh. Mom was baking something mouth-watering, one of her best recipes, but it wasn't for us. I have always resented those carrot cakes and cherry tortes that left our kitchen untasted.

> *Don't let your life speed out of control. Live intentionally. Do something today that will last beyond your lifetime.*
>
> Barbara Johnson

How about you? Who gets your best efforts? Do you spend all your creative energies on church, work, and school functions? It's so easy to let your family and friends know that they're special, too! Bake that complicated layer cake recipe! Make your top-secret broccoli salad recipe! Set the table with the good dishes! Have a picnic. Host a tea party. Blow up balloons. Buy fresh flowers. And do it all *just* for your family and friends!

9. What area in your life needs a little planning right now? As you begin the planning process, where do you see your endeavors fitting into God's will?

✦ DIGGING DEEPER ✦

This time, we have several verses from the Bible that speak about God's plans. Do you have a few different Bibles in your house? When you are looking up these verses, try reading them in several translations. Sometimes the wording in one version will simply leap off the page for you and help you to understand a passage better than you ever have before!

- Psalm 33:11
- Psalm 40:5
- Psalm 138:8
- Proverbs 16:9
- Proverbs 19:21
- Isaiah 30:1
- Jeremiah 18:12

✦ PONDER & PRAY ✦

Pray this week for God's inspiration in planning your days. Find at least one way to include God in your week—whether it's adding D.V. to your letter writing or memorizing a new passage from the Scriptures. Then, ask God to help you use your creativity to begin a new tradition in your home or at work that would please Him—whether it's reading the Narnia Chronicles out loud with your family or having a Monday morning devotional time with your coworkers.

✦ TRINKETS TO TREASURE ✦

This week's trinket will fill your days with sweet fragrances—a small bottle of body mist. The mist is to remind you our days on this earth are as fleeting as vapor (James 4:15). When you spray the perfume on yourself, you only see the mist for a few seconds and then it is gone. However, the fragrance left behind lasts for hours. Remember to plan for God's will in your days. Glorify God in your traditions. Make a place for God in each and every day, for though our days may be short, the results of our efforts will linger on, even into future generations.

✦ NOTES & PRAYER REQUESTS ✦

_____

_____

_____

_____

_____

_____

_____

_____

_____

CHAPTER 7

PRAYING FOR GOD'S WILL

"NOW THIS IS THE CONFIDENCE THAT WE HAVE
IN HIM, THAT IF WE ASK ANYTHING ACCORDING
TO HIS WILL, HE HEARS US."

1 John 5:14, NKJV

In one of my earliest memories, I am
seated close to my mother at the foot of
my bed. My toes squirmed into the lush-
ness of purple shag carpeting. My restless
fingers traced the rickrack trim on the Sunbonnet
Sue quilt sewn by my great-grandmother. Phrase by
phrase, she spoke the words to the Lord's Prayer.
Phrase by phrase, I repeated them back to her. "Our
Father, which art in heaven . . ."

Many of us learned to say certain prayers
while we were very small. Even as we learned
"Jack and Jill" and "Little Boy Blue," we
were taught to give simple thanks and make
humble petitions to God. "Now I lay me down to
sleep, I pray Thee Lord Thy child to keep . . ." Or
"Jesus, tender Shepherd, hear me; Bless Thy little
lamb tonight . . ." And "Good night! Good night! Far
flies the light . . ." We learned to sing a prayer of
thanks in the Doxology, "Praise God, from whom all

CLEARING ✦ THE ✦ COBWEBS

Do you have friends or
relatives who are
prayer warriors on
your behalf? Who
can you depend on
to uplift your needs
in prayer?

blessings flow . . ." And in "Now thank we all our God, with hearts and hands and voices . . ."

My cousins always began their meals by intoning together: "For that which we are about to receive, may we be truly thankful." We had friends in our small town who began each mealtime with a traditional prayer spoken in Swedish. I always puzzled over the rhyming in the classic "God is great, God is good, Let us thank Him for our food." And at our local greasy spoon, there was a handmade wooden sign over the counter with the brief statement "Good food. Good meat. Good Lord. Let's eat!"

1. How would you define prayer? What would you compare it to?

Every day I pray the most powerful prayer: "Lord, close the doors I don't need to walk through today. Open the doors that I do. Steer me away from people I don't need to deal with today. Put people in my path that I do. And, Lord, don't let me waste time.

Thelma Wells

2. According to the Bible, prayer is a part of God's will for our lives. In Romans, we discover that even Jesus prays for us "according to the will of God" (Rom. 8:27). Why is prayer so important?

3. While He was here on earth, Jesus prayed for His followers. Read John 17:9–16. What are some of the things Jesus asks the Father to do for His disciples?

4. It is nice to know that Jesus lifted up His companions in prayer, but it gets better. Who is Jesus praying for in John 17:20?

Today, many of us keep tabs on our prayer lives through journals in which we write our concerns, feelings, and activities culminating in a prayer that might be two lines or two pages long. I'm an occasional scribbler of thought and prayer, not a daily one. Oh, I pray daily; I just don't record daily. In fact, for years my personal scribbles were done on the backs of envelopes, napkins, and old receipts.

Patsy Clairmont

5. After the Resurrection, Jesus knew He would be returning to His Father. He could anticipate a joyous reunion, yet He knew many would miss Him terribly. He didn't want His believers to become weighed down with loneliness or to lose hope in the long years ahead of them. So He prayed for their need. What was His prayer in John 14:16?

6. Much has been made of four little letters—WWJD. Though many find it helpful to ask themselves "What would Jesus do?" it is just as important to ask ourselves "What is Jesus doing?" Read Romans 8:34 and Hebrews 7:25. What is Christ doing right now for you?

The joy and pleasure of speaking with the Lord is far superior to anything that life on this earth affords. Through prayer I become centered and serene. When I'm quiet and still, I sense the Lord comes near as I enter His presence.

Luci Swindoll

*C*an you imagine carrying on in prayer for centuries on end? Some of us have trouble keeping a prayerful attitude for more than a few minutes at a time! It gives this mind-boggling concept some perspective if we picture Christ's ministry as that of a courtroom lawyer. He is our Defender, reminding the Father our sins are forgiven. In the trial of the millennia, He stands between the accuser and us. Jesus protects our very lives by interceding on our behalf.

Yet we can also know He is watching over us, with love in His eyes, praying we will choose to obey. Jesus longs for us to pursue God's will.

7. Just as Jesus intercedes on our behalf, we should be praying for each other! Look at Colossians 4:12. At the close of this little letter, Paul encloses greetings from one of His companions to the folks back home. What does Epaphras pray?

Pray confidently. But be careful what you pray for—because everything and anything is possible through the power of prayer!

Barbara Johnson

8. Who do you pray for on a consistent basis? Have you ever prayed that they might "stand perfect and complete in all the will of God"?

9. Does the prospect of praying out loud leave you shaking in your proverbial boots? Do extreme circumstances leave you numb before the Lord, unable to form the words of a prayer? Never fear! What does Romans 8:26 tell us?

✦ DIGGING DEEPER ✦

Consider these passages on prayer. They give us a peek at the prayers those before us prayed. They provide a model for our own prayers. They inspire us to go to the Father ourselves, seeking His will.

- Matthew 5:44
- Matthew 14:23
- Luke 18:1
- John 16:26
- 1 Thessalonians 5:17
- James 5:16

✦ PONDER & PRAY ✦

Let's seek out some of the smallest prayers in the Scriptures this week. Whisper them back to God, or pray them on behalf of your friends and family. Rewrite them, personalizing them by mentioning people by name. Insert your own name into prayers of praise, letting Him hear the love in your heart!

- 1 Chronicles 21:8
- Philippians 1:9
- Colossians 1:9
- 2 Thessalonians 1:11

✦ TRINKETS TO TREASURE ✦

Prayer is at the top of most Christians' wish lists. We either want it, or we want more of it! We wish to draw closer to God in this intimate communication of the heart. We want to tell God everything that is troubling us, and know He hears us. Many of us also long to be prayer warriors on behalf of our friends and family. There is power in prayer, and our deepest longing is to lift up those around us, just like Jesus is always praying for us. With that in mind, this week's trinket is a little toy soldier. Let the very sight of this "prayer warrior" prompt you to lift up your heart to your Father in heaven.

✦ NOTES & PRAYER REQUESTS ✦

_____

_____

_____

_____

_____

_____

_____

CHAPTER 8

God's Will for Our Hearts

"In everything give thanks; for this is the will of God in Christ Jesus for you."

1 Thessalonians 5:18, NKJV

When my daughter was little, she was such a little sparkler. Her eyes had a twinkle, she loved to chatter away, and she had such a thankful attitude! With all the wonder a three-year-old could muster, she found a wealth of little things to exclaim over. The funny thing was, it didn't take much—a brand new pink crayon, a ladybug on the windowsill, a squirrel on the birdfeeder, a bracelet made from yarn, a new shape of pasta, the first dandelion of summer. "Oh, Mama!" she would shriek, startling me. I would rush to see what calamity had befallen her, only to find her in delight over some small discovery. I would dutifully ooh and aah over her newest find. Often, these became opportunities to point her little heart toward God, and offer up a prayer of thanks for His making such wonderful things for our world. Pretty soon, she was prompting us to remember her discoveries in our prayers of thanks at mealtimes and bedtimes. She was living proof of

CLEARING
✦ THE ✦
COBWEBS

Are you a stocker-upper? I mean, when you buy groceries, do you always buy extra to keep in your pantry? If you were to check in your cupboards now, how many days could you go without shopping and still provide basic meals for your household?

> *God has two dwelling places: one in heaven, and one in a thankful heart.*
>
> Barbara Johnson

the Scripture that says "Let your lives overflow with thanksgiving for all He has done!" (Col. 2:7, NLT). There is nothing quite like a child to re-open our eyes to the miracles we have gotten used to.

1. Aha! Now this is the very sort of thing we've been looking for. We have found a sentence in the Bible that is straightforward about the will of God. It is so bold in its assertion: "this *is* the will of God for you!" Just for the record, what is God's will in 1 Thessalonians 5:18?

2. So far this week, could you say you've been thankful for everything that has come your way? Why or why not?

> *If you're going through a stormy time in your life, realize with gratitude that our all-wise, loving Father hasn't deserted you. He isn't allowing you to be tossed about. He is working with awesome skill to smooth your rough edges and bring forth from your soul the brilliant loveliness of Christ.*
>
> Barbara Johnson

3. Thanksgiving is tied closely to prayer in the Scriptures. When we find ourselves overwhelmed with gratitude towards God, what could be more natural then telling Him so! What is the Psalmist thankful for in Psalm 95:1–6?

4. It is easy to be thankful once we have received the things we desire. Turn to Philippians 4:6. When does thankfulness put in its appearance here?

I have always been amazed at the children of Israel. Have you ever seen such an ungrateful lot? God frees them from their chains, drowns their pursuers, shades them with a cloud by day, provides them with a nightlight at night, brings forth water in the midst of the desert, gives them bread from heaven itself, talks one-on-one with their leader, and promises them beautiful new homes in a land that will be all theirs. What slave would have dreamed so much? But they are not thankful. Worse, they complain!

> *Wherever you are now is God's provision, not His punishment. Celebrate this moment, and try very hard to do it with conscious gratitude.*
>
> Luci Swindoll

I wonder what would have happened if the Israelites had considered their circumstances with a brighter eye, and simply said, "Thank you, Lord." Don't you fall into the trap of murmuring! God's will for our lives doesn't include griping and grumbling. We are called to an attitude of gratitude!

5. Thankfulness has a way of bubbling up. We can't help it when our hearts are full—it just overflows! What outlet of praise is mentioned in both Psalm 69:30 and Psalm 92:1?

> *I'm learning to stop for thankful moments. It's become a daily discipline of mine since I found that I was getting overwhelmed by all the daily stuff that "has to get done."*
>
> Sheila Walsh

6. Do you have a favorite song that often flows out of your thankful heart?

7. Another aspect of the thankful heart is found in 2 Corinthians 4:15. What is the result of the thanksgiving we lift up?

8. 1 Thessalonians 1:2 mentions something we should *always* be thankful for. What is that?

> *Giving thanks does wonders for my soul. It refocuses me on what's really important so that instead of dwelling on the fact that my son, Christian just tried to flush my new pale blue suede pumps down the toilet, I can celebrate the gift of a child when so many arms are empty.*
>
> Sheila Walsh

✦ DIGGING DEEPER ✦

Have you ever tried to count your blessings? Many times, our prayers of thanks to the Lord end up in a rut. "Thank You for this food . . . for our home . . . for my family . . . for this day . . ." There's no need to follow this rote. Why not boost the creativity level in your prayers of thanks this week! Get a notebook or journal, and put it somewhere where you will see it every day—by your favorite chair, on your bedside table, on your desk, in your bathroom. Then, each day, write one sentence thanking God for something. The only catch is that you can never repeat yourself. As your list of blessings grows in number, your attitude of gratitude will surely grow along with it.

✦ PONDER & PRAY ✦

It's an old saying, that every cloud has its silver lining. Days may seem bleak, and gloominess may settle over our hearts, but there is always something to be thankful for. No matter what happens in a day, look for that glittering glimpse of heaven around the edges of gray. May the Spirit bring us up short, in the middle of a murmur, and cause us to remember God's will for our hearts—thankfulness. This week, pray that the Lord will help you transform your grumblings to gratitude. Allow the love of the Lord to fill your heart with a song.

✦ TRINKETS TO TREASURE ✦

To remind us that the thankfulness in our hearts should bubble up every day, this week you are presented with bubbles—silvery, iridescent, translucent bubbles. Send them up into the air with the warmth of your breath. Watch them drift heavenwards, like songs of praise and prayers of thanksgiving. Fill the air with them, and remember how numerous God's blessings are. Make each shimmering bubble a "thank you" from your grateful heart.

✦ NOTES & PRAYER REQUESTS ✦

CHAPTER 9

GOD WANTS HOLINESS

"FOR THIS IS THE WILL OF GOD, YOUR SANCTIFICATION."

1 Thessalonians 4:3, NKJV

When I was growing up, there were three kinds of clothes in my closet. There were play clothes, there were school clothes, and then there was that one "special" dress. Play clothes were the jeans and t-shirts for working in the garden, riding my bike, and exploring the barn. School clothes were not fancy, but they were clean and neat. Mom expected them to *stay* clean and neat, so once we got home from school, they were exchanged for play clothes. But that one special dress was different. It was set apart from the rest. It was too good for play. It was too good for school. In fact, it only made an appearance at weddings, school concerts, and picture day. Between events, it stayed in the back corner of my closet, protected from dust by a plastic bag.

When an event rolled around that was deemed worthy of bringing out the special dress, I would be gussied up to match my dress. A bubble bath was drawn, curlers were set, and nails were painted. Once I was all powdered and primped, the dress would be slipped over my head and the ruffles smoothed until the dress hung just right. That kid

CLEARING
✦ THE ✦
COBWEBS

How long did it take you to get ready for a big event when you were a teenager? What were some of your rituals? Does it take you more or less time now to get all fancied up? Has your routine for preening changed over time?

in jeans who loved to swing on the tire swing in the back yard was transformed into a little princess.

I always remember that one special dress when I read about the Israelites. When holy days rolled around, God told them to get ready, and to sanctify themselves ahead of time. The call would go out, like the one in Joshua 3:5: "Sanctify yourselves, for tomorrow the Lord will do wonders among you" (NKJV). Then, the whole camp would turn into a bustle of activity. Clothes were washed (Ex. 19:14), baths were in order, and there was much combing and braiding and oiling of hair. Men would trim their beards and women would put on their jewelry. I guess that's why we have the saying that cleanliness is next to godliness!

1. Paul says that God's will for our lives includes our sanctification (1 Thess. 4:3). Sanctification is a pretty big theological-sounding word. What does it mean?

> I have a basket at my tubside filled with cleaning utensils: sponges, brushes, loofahs, pumice, and soaps. As helpful as these items are, they do not compare to how clean I feel when I have spent moments in the Lord's presence, especially when I begin with a confession time.
>
> Patsy Clairmont

2. Okay, so then what does holy mean?

3. How long has your sanctification been in God's plans? Ephesians 1:4 gives us a peek at God's timeline.

4. Why does God want us to be sanctified? Read Leviticus 11:44–45. Of course this passage refers to the Jews, God's chosen people. But, the same call is extended to Christians. What does 1 Peter 1:15 say?

> *I was in God's mind before I was ever in the womb of my mother. Specific attention, thought, and planning about me took place before God actually formed me in the womb. Not only am I a planned event, I was "set apart." We all have a specific task to do for God, and it was planned in His head before we were ever formed.*
>
> Marilyn Meberg

5. How does sanctification take place? How does God make us holy? Here are several passages that show how we are set apart.

- John 17:19
- Hebrews 10:10
- Romans 15:16
- 1 Thessalonians 5:23
- 1 Timothy 4:5
- Hebrews 10:29
- Ephesians 5:26
- Numbers 15:40

*W*e are being prepared for the biggest event in history. We are being cleaned up, decked out, and ornamented for the wedding of the millennia! Jesus is preparing His people as a bride, making sure that we can be presented without spot or blemish (Eph. 5:26). He has dressed us with garments of salvation and clothes of righteousness. We are like a bride, adorned with jewels (Is. 61: 10).

God is using His Word, His Spirit, Christ's blood, prayer, and all the rest to cleanse us, to robe us, to adorn us. It is part of His will for your life to have you undergo this sanctification. All this Bible study, prayer, and the living out of our faith is making the bride of Christ more and more beautiful. Your quiet times with God are better than beauty sleep, a trip to the hairdresser, and a day at the spa combined!

6. What happens when we are sanctified? Are we like that "special" dress, hanging in the corner of the closet, too good for everyday use? Of course not! According to 2 Timothy 2:21, what do we become?

> *Every day we must renew our minds. Right now is our only opportunity to live for Him. Treat this moment, right now, as if it's your last moment, because it might be. Yesterday's blessings and progresses are not today's. Be kind today. Lift up the Lord today. Share something with someone today.*
>
> Thelma Wells

7. According to Titus 2:14, God redeemed us and purified us as His own special people. What are we ready for?

8. Lastly, we find a verse with a twist on sanctification. What does the first part of 1 Peter 3:15 urge us to do?

✦ Digging Deeper ✦

The Bible uses the idea of washing to help us understand sanctification. Look at these different passages that talk about being cleansed. Then post them in the bathroom, and memorize them as you wash!

- Psalm 51:2, 7
- 1 Corinthians 6:11
- Isaiah 1:16
- Jeremiah 4:14
- John 13:8
- Acts 22:16
- Titus 3:5

✦ Ponder & Pray ✦

Sanctification is always a life-long process, and thankfully the Lord allows us to tackle our down-falls one at a time. The Holy Spirit often convicts us of one thing, helps us to wrestle its roots from our lives and give it over to God, only to point out some "new" sin we hadn't seen before. Pray this week that the Lord would open your eyes to His next renovation project. Then ask God to give you the humility to accept the truth and a teachable heart toward the changes you must make. But don't stop there, all cleaned up with no place to go. Seek the good works He has for you, then do them with zeal!

✦ Trinkets to Treasure ✦

With all this talk of washing and cleansing, your gift for this week was an easy one to choose—a bar of soap. Work up a lather as you consider your sanctification this week, and repeat these words of David every time you wash your hands. "Wash me and I shall be whiter than snow" (Ps. 51:7). Then, when you have patted your hands dry, lift them to your nose and take a deep breath. For a few moments, anyhow, your hands are as clean as they can get. Then, as you return to your day's tasks, recall to mind that you are prepared for a task—whatever purpose the Lord may have for you.

✦ Notes & Prayer Requests ✦

CHAPTER 10

REST CONTENT

"THE FEAR OF THE LORD LEADS TO LIFE: THEN ONE RESTS CONTENT, UNTOUCHED BY TROUBLE."

Proverbs 19:23

With a sigh, I head for the laundry room, where my cleaning caddy and rags are kept. This is not my favorite way to start a day. One child's bed was soaked, and the washing machine is already chugging away. Another child seems to have come down with something, and I'll need a bucket to save the cream-colored carpeting from a stain where he threw up his orange juice. My husband breezes past, freshly showered and dressed for his day in the office. He gets a weak smile and a limp wave as I trudge past with ammonia scenting the air around me. I wish I could trade places with him right now! Oh, to be clean. Oh, to have a tidy little cubicle to escape to.

A mother's lot in life is certainly not a glamorous one. Our clothing is covered in mysterious stains, and we barely have time for a shower. We are asked to do the same menial tasks over and over again, with no end in sight. We do the dirtywork, cleaning up everything from mud to mucus. We long for adult conversation. Every step we

CLEARING ✦ THE ✦ COBWEBS

Most of us are either working outside the home now, or did at some point in our lives. Do you like your job or dread it? What's your favorite perk? What's the biggest drawback?

make towards neatness and organization is quickly undone by small hands and feet. It's pretty easy to feel sorry for ourselves!

In circumstances like these, it can be difficult to feel contented. In the midst of the mundane, can we find joy and satisfaction?

1. Another day, another chance to make peanut butter and jelly sandwiches and pour glasses of milk. What does Ecclesiastes 3:13 say about our lunch-making efforts?

> *As a single person with no children, let me say I believe life's highest calling is motherhood. An endeavor like no other, it demands a sense of selflessness that must be renewed every day.*
>
> Luci Swindoll

2. The loads of laundry that are always waiting for us, the lawn that needs mowing, the bills that need paying, the long hours at the office, the hour-long commutes, the loading of the dishwasher—in short, all our work—is a gift from God! How can work be a gift?

3. That Ecclesiastes passage also says that God wants all people to be happy in their work. When I have to head for the plunger, a mop, and a bucket, joy isn't necessarily the feeling that overwhelms my soul! Are you more of an "eager beaver" or a "disgruntled employee" for the Lord?

4. I used to think that life would be so much easier if I just had a dishwasher. I was sure that with that particular appliance in my kitchen, "life would be a dream, sweetheart!" What one thing are you waiting for to make things better for you, and once you get that one thing, your work would be more pleasant?

We have good days, great days, and way-down-deep-in-the-pit days. Some seasons are easier than others, while some are downright impossible. I've wondered how some folks have survived the many hardships that have come their way. Others' lives have seemed almost charmed. For each of us, our days are unpredictable, and we tip the scales from preposterous to precious. Life is a gift bulging with mystery, intrigue, comedy, tragedy—and purpose.

Patsy Clairmont

5. How would you define contentment?

6. What does Paul tell us to aspire to? Where is the scripture for this?

7. So what's the problem? Why do we need something more? Check out Hebrews 13:5 for the root to the problem.

Life is mostly doing our jobs whether we feel like it or not. But there is the secret: As we do the thing in front of us, joy comes.

Barbara Johnson

*Y*ou've heard of the tooth fairy, right? Well, my sister is always seeking the aid of "The Laundry Fairy." Now this is no little tinker-bell with wings and a wand. Actually, Laundry Fairy is one of my mother's nicknames. Whenever my sister went home for a visit, she'd drop a couple of laundry baskets on the floor in the corner of the kitchen. By the time she was ready to go home in the evening, the laundry was not only clean, but folded neatly back into the baskets. Amazing! Our kids just take it for granted that food appears in the refrigerator, clean clothes appear in their closets, and gas appears in the car's gas tank.

For many of us, our daily routine doesn't seem to make any difference. Nobody gives a thought to who changes the toilet paper rolls, puts toner in the copy machine, fills the ice cube trays, or files the receipts. And since these jobs seem unimportant, we feel unimportant.

8. Paul lived a pretty thankless life as a church planter. In fact, he held down two jobs some of the time, just to keep the money flowing while starting up a new church. What was his attitude about contentment? It's found in Philippians 4:11.

It is easy to believe that God can use our lives when we see immediate results, when positive feedback encourages us to push on. It is hard to keep walking when we see little sign that what we are doing is making a difference.

Sheila Walsh

9. One last passage about contentment. Look up 1 Timothy 6:6. What does Paul say here?

✦ DIGGING DEEPER ✦

God promises us that we can be satisfied. Even when our world feels very small and very insignificant, we can rest contented, knowing that God has His purposes for every season in our lives. Let's explore some verses that speak to our hearts about the satisfaction that can only be found in the Lord.

- Psalm 36:8
- Psalm 90:14
- Psalm 107:9
- Psalm 145:16
- Isaiah 58:11

✦ PONDER & PRAY ✦

Are you satisfied with your lot in life? Are you content? Have you decided to "bloom where you're planted"? Pray this week that God will encourage you by showing how important all the little things you do really are. Ask Him for the strength to do that thing that is in front of you. Even if your day is filled with mundane things, allow God to open your eyes to the people around you. Pray that God will inspire you with ways to add sparkle to somebody else's existence—it will certainly brighten yours!

✦ TRINKETS TO TREASURE ✦

Everywhere we look, people are trying to tell us that their products or services will make us happy. They sell their wares with "satisfaction guaranteed." Well, God says "I will always guide you and satisfy you with good things" (Is. 58:11, TEV). So this week's little doo-dad is a reminder of that fact—stickers that boldly declare "Satisfaction Guaranteed." Don't be led astray by the world's false advertising campaigns. We may not always understand what our Heavenly Father does for our own good, but we can rest contented. He will satisfy our souls with good things.

✦ Notes & Prayer Requests ✦

CHAPTER 11

SILENCE THE FOOLS

"FOR THIS IS THE WILL OF GOD, THAT BY DOING GOOD YOU MAY PUT TO SILENCE THE IGNORANCE OF FOOLISH MEN."

1 Peter 2:15, NKJV

When it comes to compliments, sometimes you have to know the complimenter in order to understand the compliment. The gushing saleswoman, who drops the word *fabulous* into her sentences with alarming frequency, should be pretty much ignored when she says that you look fabulous in the dress you're trying on. On the other hand, a reserved person's "it's okay" can speak volumes. Remember the farmer in *Babe*? At the end of the movie, when the little pig had won a great sheep-herding event, the laconic Farmer Hoggit turns to the pig and simply says "That'll do, Pig." My own father's favorite complimentary phrase is "Ya done good."

Good. Seems like such a bland word, really. The compliment with "good" in it seems lackluster when held up to ones containing "marvelous," "wonderful," and "splendid." Good seems to rank somewhere between "nice" and "okay." But the Bible is rather clear that "good" is a very special word. In fact, there is only One who *is* good (Matt. 19:17), and the rest of us don't make the grade!

CLEARING
✦ THE ✦
COBWEBS

Are you a people watcher? What kinds of things have you seen people do when they thought no one was looking?

1. God is the only one who *is* good, but we can do good. Give some examples of good things.

2. Why are we able to do good things? Matthew 12:35 gives us a clue.

3. The choice between doing good and doing evil may seem like a no-brainer. Even non-Christians like to think of themselves as "basically good people." Look at Matthew 5:44–48 and Luke 6:33. How are our choices made difficult?

> Being touched by God's extravagant grace ignites something within us that causes people to notice. It's an interior glow that is like an exterior light in that it casts its influence in spite of the degree of darkness in which it finds itself—not only in spite of the darkness but also because of it. In the darkness the light becomes more attractive, more influential, more valuable, and more obvious.
>
> Patsy Clairmont

4. Sometimes it is easier to choose the right things when there is some incentive involved. Is there a reward for doing good? Is it worth the effort to choose the good? Look at Matthew 25:21.

5. Peter says that it is God's will for us to do good. Why?

6. Daniel was a man of integrity. No one could bring an accusation against him, so they had to make one up! Proverbs 29:10 says that "the bloodthirsty hate the blameless." Most folks resent the woman who seems to have it all together. She *must* be too good to be true. What does 1 Peter 2:20 say about maintaining our integrity in the face of scrutiny?

No amount of work will enable you to inherit eternal life. But works count for something. Ain't that good news! James 1:12 says, "Blessed is the man who perseveres under trial, because when he has stood the test, he will receive the crown of life that God has promised to those who love Him." I'm excited just thinking about that pageant of crowns I can qualify for if I work the works of Him who sent me.

Thelma Wells

*I*t always amazes me what people will do in a moving vehicle. Though they're surrounded by windows on all sides, somehow folks don't realize that everybody can see them. I've seen men shaving, women putting on mascara, diaper changes in progress. Kisses are exchanged, curlers are removed, noses are picked, heated arguments are underway—all in plain view. Though this can be an endless source of amusement for people-watchers, it serves as a reminder to us all. Our lives are lived right out in the open, and people notice how we behave ourselves. Let's pray that even those we won't ever meet will be touched by the kindnesses we show one another. After all, they will know we are Christians by our love (John 13:35)!

7. No matter where we may be, somebody might just be watching us! This need not alarm us. In fact, Jesus depended upon that fact! What does He command in Matthew 5:16?

> The people around you are taking notes on your life. I know you think that they may not be noticing, but they jotted down exactly how you reacted when you had to stand in the long line, when you had to drive in the heavy traffic, when you had to deal with the difficult person, when the elevator didn't arrive in time. They've been taking notes on you. And they'll make reference back to them.
>
> Patsy Clairmont

8. Peter gives women a fine model for living in 1 Peter 3:1–6. We are called "daughters of Sarah" when we do good. What kind of things does Peter encourage Christian women to emulate?

✦ DIGGING DEEPER ✦

As Chistian women, we are challenged to follow the examples of the men and women on the pages of our Bibles. Job, Ruth, Daniel, Joseph, Paul, and Timothy are all admired for their integrity in the face of difficulties. Let's look over some passages from the Bible that speak about a blameless life.

- Psalm 37:27
- Proverbs 11:20
- Proverbs 13:6
- Ephesians 1:4
- Philippians 2:15
- Colossians 1:22
- 2 Peter 3:14

✦ PONDER & PRAY ✦

These next several days, consider yourself carefully. Does your walk match your talk? Are you living in a way that would silence your accusers? Ask God to help you live blamelessly. Also, pray for God to give you a great compassion this week. Look at your husband, your relatives, your children, your friends, your neighbors, your co-workers, the strangers you pass on the road, and the few folks you would rather just avoid through *His* eyes. Pray for a genuineness that doesn't play favorites. After all, your life may be the one that makes them long for God!

✦ TRINKETS TO TREASURE ✦

This week we have discovered that God has asked us to do *good*. This call encompasses all of our lives—our relationships with family, friends, strangers, and enemies. This integrity of life will point those around us to God. Since Jesus calls our lives a light, let's hand out our trinkets and strike up a familiar tune. Light your candles this week and hum "This Little Light of Mine."

✦ NOTES & PRAYER REQUESTS ✦

CHAPTER 12

DON'T GIVE UP!

"FOR YOU HAVE NEED OF ENDURANCE, SO THAT AFTER YOU HAVE DONE THE WILL OF GOD, YOU MAY RECEIVE THE PROMISE."

Hebrews 10:36, NKJV

We are probably all familiar with the concept that the Christian life is a race. You know: "Let us run with endurance the race that is set before us" (Heb. 12:1) and "I have fought the good fight, I have finished the race, I have kept the faith" (2 Tim. 4:7). And of course "Do you not know that those who run in a race all run, but one receives the prize? Run in such a way that you may obtain it" (1 Cor. 9:24). The gist of these passages is usually distilled into a plea for stick-to-itiveness, discipline, and endurance. Well, I'll never forget the Sunday when my pastor re-defined the race for me!

Somehow, I had lived with the impression that I needed to press on ahead of those around me. I wanted to be the one who received the prize. Compared to some people I had met, I was doing great. I could impress God by running faster. I would prove that I had more discipline, more endurance. When others fell by the wayside, my pace just looked better and better.

That's where I had it all wrong. You see, our Christian "race" isn't a competition between fellow

CLEARING ✦ THE ✦ COBWEBS

Have you ever finished a project that took a really long time—sewing a quilt, organizing your files, making scrapbooks from a pile of pictures, renovating a room, memorizing a chapter from the Bible, a big presentation at work? What was your big job, how long did it take, and how did it feel when you finally completed the task?

believers to see who can be more spiritual. God doesn't give out gold, silver, and bronze medals at the finish line. We run *together*. My pastor asked us to picture our little congregation as a pack, all bunched together and jogging along as a group. When somebody trips, the whole pack stops to lift that one up before picking up speed again. When one member grows weary under their load and begins to stumble, others come alongside to support them and help them carry their burden. We are here to help each other along towards the goal. That's why God gave us each other.

1. Who do you count as partners in this "race" of the Christian life? Name a few of the fellow-believers that are in your little corner of the whole church.

2. The writer of Hebrews says "You have need of endurance" (Heb. 10:36, NKJV). Why does doing the will of God require endurance?

If you have days when you wonder where God is showing up, think about the believers He has placed in your life to influence you in a godly way. Give Him thanks for these evidences of His work in your life. Godly friends are one of God's simple gifts to us.

Thelma Wells

3. How have the people you named earlier helped you to endure? How can you help them along life's journey?

4. What happens to folks who don't hang in there? Mark 4:17 gives us a picture of those who did not endure.

5. Paul encourages Timothy to endure, no matter what. What was Paul's earthly motivation for enduring (it's in 2 Timothy 2:10) and then his heavenly motivation for enduring (it's two verses later in 2 Timothy 2:12)?

> *Perhaps there is little immediate satisfaction in what you have been called to do, but if you will faithfully push on through the night the Lord is the one who carries a reward in His hands.*
>
> Sheila Walsh

6. If anyone would seem to have "arrived" at Christian maturity, it was Paul. But what was Paul's attitude? Philippians 3:12 shows us his heart.

Nothing lasts the way it used to in the "good old days." At least, that's what I am always hearing. When we rented a little old house from the little old man who lived next door, we were blessed with the use of his old stove. It was a huge, enamel contraption—the size and color of Moby Dick. We were stunned to learn that the sweet little couple next door had purchased it the year they had been married, and they had just celebrated their golden wedding anniversary.

That fifty-year-old appliance had hung in there through the years like a trooper! During the time when I used that old stove, I went through two vacuum cleaners, two toasters, three hand mixers, and a popcorn popper. In this hasty society, with our throwaway mentality, I don't want to break down like my long line of mixers. I want to endure like my big old behemoth of a stove!

There is just something about knowing that my failures, others' failures, hardships, mistakes, losses, and pain have meaning. For me, that understanding eases some of the agony of life and encourages me to keep on keeping on.

Patsy Clairmont

7. How does James describe Christians who are able to endure? Look in James 5:11.

8. Have you ever just wanted to give up? Did your work in the church ever leave you burned out? Does your job wear you down? Why do you think burnout happens?

Consider this as a rule of thumb: God never calls without enabling us. In other words, if He calls you to do something, He makes it possible for you to do it. And, let me go a step further: if you don't sense His strength and ability within you to do it, I would question the call.

Luci Swindoll

9. Paul gives two messages of encouragement to his churches about pressing on in the Christian walk. They are in Galatians 6:9 and 2 Thessalonians 3:13. What does he say?

✦ DIGGING DEEPER ✦

Jesus' parable of the sower describes those who do not endure in their faith as those who did not take root. There are several passages that refer to being rooted. Look these verses up and explore their descriptions of a life that is properly grounded.

- Jeremiah 17:8
- Ephesians 3:17
- Proverbs 12:3, 12
- Colossians 2:7

✦ PONDER & PRAY ✦

Seek the Lord in His Word this week, and pray that He would help you to put down deep roots. Ask the Lord to give you some gumption. Pray for enough strength to do everything that lies in your path, so that you can continue to move forward. He will supply your needs, and enable you to hang in there. Look around you this week to see who is running alongside you in the race, and find ways to lift their burdens and help them along their journey.

✦ TRINKETS TO TREASURE ✦

This last little gift is something for you to share with your particular "pack" as you run the race together, urging one another to hang in there and not give up. It's a pack of gum. When the days grow long and your energy is flagging, something as small as a piece of gum can help you perk up and keep plodding away. It's a burst of minty freshness or a sugary bubblegum boost. So unwrap a stick of gum, and pray for stick-to-itiveness in following God's will. Then offer a piece to your Christian sister, because she just might need that little lift as well.

✦ Notes & Prayer Requests ✦

✦ Shall We Review? ✦

Every chapter has added a new trinket to your treasure trove of memories. Let's remind ourselves of the lessons they hold for us!

1. Clay Pot

God's will equals *God's* will! Compared to our great God, we are humble little pots, made from clay. Yet, He has chosen to pour His riches and glory into our lives.

2. Ring

God's will is for a relationship with us, and the band we slip onto our fingers reminds us of the One who loves us more than words can possibly tell.

3. Golden Arrow

A reminder of the direction we should be choosing, even in the smallest decisions of our everyday lives.

4. Garbage Can

It's "garbage in, garbage out." While God is at work, transforming our lives, there can be a real clash of the wills. For our minds to be renewed, we must fill them with things that are pure, lovely, and true.

5. Heart Magnet

In the midst of all the things we could pursue, choose to chase after God whole-heartedly. Let your heart be drawn to God just like that magnet clings to the fridge.

5. Body Mist

Our lives are like a fleeting mist, but by planning for God's will in our days, the sweet fragrance of our lives will linger on, even to future generations.

7. Toy Soldier

God's will for our lives includes prayer. Our little "prayer warrior" reminds us that not only is Jesus praying for you right now, but we can be supporting one another in prayer as well.

8. Bubbles

God's will is a grateful heart. Fill the air with shimmering bubbles, and make each one a song of praise and a prayer of thanks for the blessings God has given you.

9. Soap

God is washing you, cleansing your heart, and making you holy. This clean-up is His preparation process for all the good things He has planned for us to do.

10. "Satisfaction Guaranteed"

Stick this label anywhere you need a reminder. God wants us to find satisfaction in our daily tasks, and joy in the work laid before us. Work is a gift from God, and we can discover contentment in our daily situations.

11. Candle

With the tune "This Little Light of Mine" running through our minds, we recall that God has called us to shine forth with integrity. You never know who is watching you! By doing good, those around us will be drawn to God.

12. Pack of Gum

As we run the race set before us, we depend upon God for the stick-to-itiveness to hang in there. Then, we look to the fellow believers who are running alongside us, and offer them a piece as well. We run in a pack, we help each other along the way, and we finish together!

✦ LEADER'S GUIDE ✦

Chapter 1

Clearing the Cobwebs: The dictionary defines willfulness as "obstinately bent on having one's own way." On the other hand, willingness is "ready to act; eagerly compliant; ungrudging acceptance." In spiritual terms, a woman characterized by willfulness would be self-centered, stiff-necked, stubborn, complaining, rebellious, and just plain sinful. However, a woman with a heart of willingness would be teachable, flexible, ready to serve, content, and even joyful! Pray that God would give you a willing heart!

1. All of us have our bouts with the "Terrible Twos" in our Christian walk. When things don't go our way, we can be reduced to pouting, mood swings, whining, grumbling, murmuring, tantrums, and tears. Unlike the distraught mother, God does not budge. Thankfully, God's Spirit takes all this emotional venting in stride, and when we have calmed down a bit, His still, small voice brings us back into a more contrite frame of mind.

2. So many answers are possible here. We do not have God's divine perspective— only He has the big picture. Our emotions tend to rule our decisions—only He does good all the time. We despair when our troubles overwhelm us—only God can see how these trials are transforming our character.

3. Answers here will be varied. We might have a bone to pick with God about our jobs, our looks, our personality traits, our husbands, our children, our parents, our financial status, our unanswered prayers, our sharp tongues, our disappointments, our addictions, our expectations, our abilities, our peace of mind, or our joy.

4. In the New Living Translation, it says that (1) the Potter has the right to decide what kind of pot to make with His lumps of clay. Some of us will be beautiful decorations, but some of us will be trash bins. Paul also says that (2) God has the right to exercise His judgment. (3) He has the right to exercise His power. (4) God has the right to be patient with those who are on the path to destruction. And best of all, (5) God has the right to pour out the riches of His glory on us, who have been given mercy. I guess you could say that God can do just as He pleases!

5. Sometimes it helps to look at a Scripture verse in another translation. In the New Century Version, this same verse reads "God is working in you to help you want to do and be able to do what pleases Him." God is able to change our hearts so that we want to do those things that will bring Him glory! It becomes our desire to do His will. Then, he enables us to follow through. He enables us to do His will as well.

6. Romans 12:2 says, "then you will be able to know the will of God—what is good and pleasing to Him and is perfect" (TEV). God's will is whatever He wants. If He were a spoiled child, that could be terrible and terrifying. Thankfully, His will is always good and pleasing and perfect!

7. "This is the will of the Father who sent Me, that of all He has given Me I should lose nothing, but should raise it up at the last day" (John 6:39, NKJV). It is God's will for us to be saved. Jesus will be faithful to raise up His own.

Chapter 2

Clearing the Cobwebs: Many different people in our lives can influence our initial understanding of who God is and what He wants for us—a parent, grandparent, Sunday school teacher, pastor, youth leader, Bible study leader, close relative, friend, mentor. Have you ever considered how you might be used to help those around you in their walks? Someone might just be taking notes on you!

1. Everyone's answers will be different here, for each of us has very different needs. How very miraculous that God knows us so very well, and His relationship with each of us meets us right where we are. God's love is so deep and so personal, there is no need for sibling rivalry within the Christian family!

2. Mark 3:35 says "Whoever does the will of God is My brother and My sister and mother." When we become Christians, we are welcomed into God's family. He calls us "joint heirs with Jesus" (Rom. 8:17) and reminds us that we have been adopted (Rom. 8:15). We are sisters of the Savior, and someday He will welcome us into the mansions He has prepared for us. Heaven will be like a big family reunion. What a homecoming it will be!

3. Believing God is not simply understanding things with your head. Faith is not just a fact-finding tour. Knowledge is a starting point, but it cannot be the stopping point. James says to believe God's commandments and yet not act upon them is a sure sign of a dead faith (James 2:17). Jesus says "if you love Me, keep My commandments" (Matt. 15:10). Believe Jesus, and let what you believe transform your life! Live out your faith!

4. A church sign in our neighborhood had a new quip this week: "Everybody wants to go to heaven, but nobody wants to obey God." I once heard a pastor say if we really believed what Jesus told us, we would be a changed people. Christianity is not about church attendance, potluck suppers, and Christmas plays. This is serious business, and souls hang in the balance! Take a long look at what God is telling you in His Word and really believe it. See if it doesn't change you.

5. 1 Timothy 2:4 says that "[God] desires all men to be saved and to come to the knowledge of the truth." God wants us to know Him. He wants us to seek Him out. He has promised to reveal Himself to those who seek Him (Deut. 4:29). This is a wonderful promise for us, but it also gives us hope for those unsaved friends we have been praying for. It is God's desire that they be saved, too!

6. Like the little, lost sheep that strayed from the other ninety-nine, we sometimes wander from God's side. Yet we are so precious in His sight He chases after us, not willing to lose even one of His flock. Matthew 18:14 says, "It is not the will of your Father in heaven that one of these little ones should perish." God does not want to lose you!

7. God isn't being slow just to stir up impatience on our part. It's pretty clear that He's being merciful! He is patiently waiting, giving people more time to repent. Ladies, this means we have a little more time to let our friends, neighbors, and relatives know about this wonderful Savior who loves them and has a plan for their life.

8. Jeremiah 29:11 says "'For I know the plans I have for you,' says the Lord. 'They are plans for good and not for disaster, to give you a future and a hope.'" These words bring so much comfort and confidence because we can rest in the promise that God does have a plan for us, and that it is a good one. We may not understand our current predicaments, but we know we have a hope and a future.

9. Paul talks about his calling in 1 Corinthians 1:1: "Paul, called to be an apostle of Jesus Christ through the will of God." He recognized he was in a place of ministry because it was God's will for his life. Paul had a proper perspective, understanding he had not achieved so much for the sake of Christianity in his own power. What had been accomplished was through God's enabling and for God's glory.

10. It is very important to remember our calling, and even our gifts, can change throughout the various seasons of life. A young mother might feel trapped in the nursery, but the lessons she learns there may develop her budding gifts of wisdom and discernment. Some years might find us at the forefront, leading and teaching. Other times, we slip from the public eye, serving as advisors and intercessors. No one is better than the other, for every aspect brings glory to God!

Chapter 3

1. Since the Bible is the inspired Word of God, it is in no danger of becoming outdated or antiquated. Rather, it is living and powerful (Heb. 4:12). We have the assurance that His divine power has given us all the things we need for life and godliness (2 Pet. 1:3). You can apply biblical principles to your decision-making process, knowing His "advice" is good and right and true.

2. In John 15:8–12, Jesus urges His followers to do several things: become His disciples, bear fruit, obey His commands, and love one another. The results of this lifestyle are magnificent: abiding in His love and having complete joy! The Scriptures are filled with these kinds of promises—the ones where God says "if you will do this, I will do this for you." Get yourself a colored pencil and start underlining these precious words of life. Then you will know what God wants!

3. Hmmm. Trick question, I think. Of course the Bible isn't just anything. We cannot limit something that is "living and powerful and sharper than a two-edged sword" to the guidebook shelf of our library. That really isn't its purpose. God gave us His Word in order to reveal Himself to us. However, in the process of speaking to us through His Word, God does guide us as we follow after Him. He leads us!

4. It's hard to put a finger on how God leads us along. Sometimes, things just seem to work out! Often, a path appears through seemingly impossible circumstances. Sometimes, a thing just feels right. At other times, we just don't have peace in our hearts about a decision. We need to prayerfully pay attention to those inner promptings and to our circumstances. These are the things God can use to help us make our choices.

5. Everyone's answer will vary here, for it is a personal question. Most often, advice is sought from a pastor, mentor, teacher, one's parents, grandparents, or trusted friends.

6. Today's English Version of the Bible phrases the proverbs very bluntly when it states: "Stupid people always think they are right. Wise people listen to advice" (Prov. 12:5). When you are troubled by a decision you must make, don't allow your questions to overwhelm you. Seek out the counsel of someone you trust—someone who loves you. God might just use them to speak to you!

7. The New Century Version says: "So what was the law for? It was given to show the wrong things people do are against God's will" (Gal. 3:19). By setting the standard, God's laws establish the line between right and wrong. Wrongdoing is against God's will. Obedience is God's will. He is glorified when our choices are in line with His will.

8. Ephesians 2:3 describes our fallen state: "we all once conducted ourselves in the lusts of our flesh, fulfilling the desires of our flesh and of the mind" (NKJV). But now we do not cater to every whim and selfish urge. Paul warns against being ruled by our appetites: "I discipline my body and bring it into subjection, lest . . . I myself should become disqualified" (1 Cor. 9:27, NKJV).

9. "We know our old life died with Christ on the Cross so our sinful selves would have no power over us and we would not be slaves to sin. Anyone who has died is made free from sin's control" (Rom. 6:6–7, NCV). We have power from God to do the right thing. He enables us to do His will! We are free of sin's control. Do you believe it?

Chapter 4

1. "Now the works of the flesh are evident, which are: adultery, fornication, uncleanness, lewdness, idolatry, sorcery, hatred, contentions, jealousies, outbursts of wrath, selfish ambitions, dissensions, heresies, envy, murders, drunkenness, revelries, and the like" (Gal. 5:19–21, NKJV).

2. "The fruit of the Spirit is love, joy, peace, longsuffering, kindness, goodness, faithfulness, gentleness, self-control" (Gal. 5:22–23, NKJV). If we are living lives characterized by the fruit of the Spirit, not only will God be glorified . . . we will be nice to be around!

3. It doesn't take much to stand out nowadays. Patience, concern, and an understanding attitude go a long way in a busy store, a long line, or on the freeway. People notice a warm smile, a compliment, and a willingness to listen as marks of uncommon courtesy.

4. "For I have come down from heaven, not to do My own will, but the will of Him who sent Me." (John 6:38, NKJV). Jesus had come to this earth with a mission. Though confronted with temptations and His own human emotions, He never lost that focus. He knew there was a divine purpose behind everything that was happening to Him. He moved through life with a surety that His Father's way was best.

5. "He no longer should live the rest of his time in the flesh for the lusts of men, but for the will of God" (1 Pet. 4:2, NKJV). Peter says that we should live for the will of God! Imagine living every hour of every day with that purpose always before us. We would be transformed by that kind of focus!

6. "Do not change yourselves to be like the people of this world, but be changed within by a new way of thinking. Then you will be able to decide what God wants for you; you will know what is good and pleasing to Him and what is perfect" (Rom. 12:2, NCV). As another translation puts it, we must be "transformed by the renewing of our minds" (NKJV).

7. Many Christians have amazing testimonies of the transformation that God made in their lives the very hour they were saved. For most of us, though, Christ is working in us over the course of days, months, and even years. The renewing process is ongoing, and at times frustrating. It isn't always easy, and it won't happen overnight. The promise is that He's faithful to complete what He has begun!

8. "My friends, fill your minds with those things that are good and that deserve praise: things that are true, noble, right, pure, lovely and honorable" (Phil. 4:8, TEV). The old adage "garbage in; garbage out" is only too true. We are subtly influenced by what surrounds us. A good friend might lead us nearer to God, but we can easily be drawn down into a spiral of gossip, backbiting, time-wasting, indulgence, busyness, and excess. Are you spending too much time with people who only bring out the worst in you? Take a careful look at the other areas that input into your mind: books, magazines, television, radio, movies, music, and the Internet. Does their influence far outweigh God's on your life?

9. Transformation is not in our own power or strength—it is an act of grace. God will transform us, for "we are His workmanship" (Eph. 2:10, NKJV).

Chapter 5

1. Those of us who enjoy a pretty serious hobby or other interest find it hard to pass on certain things: cookbooks, garage sales, fabric stores, used book shops, garden nurseries, kitchen gadgets, etc. We are drawn, as if by some invisible force, to the pursuit of our particular passion. These are outlets of our God-given creativity, and add interest and beauty to our lives.

2. The Spirit of God inside us is always stirring up our heart with an eagerness for the things of the Lord. We feel Him drawing us toward His Word and toward prayer. We get excited when we grasp some truth for the first time. We long to study the Bible, and understand God more thoroughly. He also inspires within us a love for others that may not have been there before, and a desire for these people to also know God.

3. "Do the will of God with all your heart" (Eph. 6:6, NLT). Finding God's will cannot be a halfhearted pursuit for the Christian. We are to be wholehearted, enthusiastic, unreserved, and unqualified in seeking God's path!

4. We have all experienced those times when we lose ourselves in something we love. Time slips away when we are engrossed in a good book, puttering in the garden, browsing through pattern books, or visiting with friends. Then, there are the dreaded tasks that get put off until we force ourselves to take care of them—scrubbing the bathtub, returning phone calls at work, emptying the litter box, paying the bills, cleaning the oven, dusting the ceiling fan, preparing for that presentation, defrosting the freezer.

5. Do everything "heartily, as to the Lord" (KJV). Imagine the thrill of standing someday before the Lord and hearing Him say "well done, good and faithful servant." Isn't it worth some of the dailyness of life to know God is pleased?

6. "Now, Israel, this is what the Lord your God wants you to do: Respect the Lord your God and do what He has told you to do. Love Him. Serve the Lord with your whole being" (Deut. 10:12, NCV). Simplify these commands by just looking at the verbs involved here: we are to respect, do, love, and serve!

7. "The thing you should want most is God's kingdom and doing what God wants. Then all these other things you need will be given to you" (Matt. 6:33, NCV). When we try to do everything in life on our own timetable and with our own strength, we are bound to flounder and fail. It is only when God is first in our lives that the rest falls into place behind. Let's start our mornings with the tune of "Seek Ye First" in our hearts and on our lips!

8. "And you shall love the Lord your God with all your heart, with all your soul, with all your mind, and with all your strength. This is the first commandment" (Mark 12:30, NKJV).

9. When we talk about our hearts, we usually mean our emotions, our impulses, and our deepest desires. Our minds bring in the thoughts, plans, creativity, hopes, and dreams. Our strength would include our efforts, energies, and our time. God longs for us to give all of these aspects of our self to Him.

Chapter 6

1. Those of us who are planners are able to map out ways to reach out and touch our sisters' hearts. We make the sign-up sheets, plan the workdays, organize the secret sisters clubs, and we can be depended on to stick to the schedule. God also uses those of us who are spontaneous sisters. We drop in on our friends, buy silly little gifts, host picnics in the park, and make encouraging phone calls. One way is not the right way, nor is one style better than the other. God uses both for His glory.

2. Planning helps us keep on track, maintain our focus, and achieve our goals. Planning for God's will can be as simple as allowing time in our daily schedule for Bible reading and prayer. By further investing the time to set up a routine to our days, we bless our families and ourselves with some much-needed stability. By guarding against a hurry-scurry lifestyle, we are able to stay true to God's will in the little decisions and choices we face every day.

3. "'I know what I am planning for you,' says the Lord. 'I have good plans for you, not plans to hurt you. I will give you hope and a good future'" (Jer. 29:11, NCV). Though we cannot always see God's hand in our lives, His plans are unfolding all around us. We can rest in the confidence that in the end, the plans are for our good, and we have hope.

4. "When it was clear that we couldn't persuade him, we gave up and said, 'The will of the Lord be done'" (Acts 21:14, NLT). When faced with Paul's conviction that God was indeed leading him in this unlikely direction, his Christian friends gave up their arguments. Sure, they had common sense on their side. Sure, it was hard to give up their own wishes in this decision. But, they stopped begging Paul to change his mind. They gave him up into God's care, and said "God's will be done."

5. "One of the things I always pray for is the opportunity, God willing, to come at last to see you" (Rom. 1:10, NLT). The same phrase is dropped into Paul's story again in Acts 18:21.

6. "You do not know what will happen tomorrow. For what is your life? It is even a vapor that appears for a little time and then vanishes away. Instead you ought to say, 'If the Lord wills, we shall live and do this or that'" (James 4:13–15, NKJV). James encourages believers to remember that God's will should be the focus of our plans.

Getting wrapped up in everyday business decisions and housekeeping can make us forget that life is both changeable and fleeting—like vapor. We must keep the main thing the main thing, or risk frittering our time away. The Lord's will should be foremost in our minds.

7. Many of us have set goals for ourselves. "By the first of the year, I want to see this accomplished." Or we categorize tasks and goals into one-year, five-year, and ten-year plans. By assessing these grand schemes from God's perspective, we often discover that the things that are most important to Him have been completely left out! Make sure your goals don't just include home repairs, job promotions, family trips, weight loss, and landscaping. Remember to include God-honoring goals in your life— befriending unsaved neighbors, reading through the Bible in one year, Scripture memorization, and short-term missions trips are worth considering!

8. We are creatures of habit, so for better or for worse, we fall into some kind of pattern. These become traditions that help give structure and familiarity to our days. Remember when you were a kid, how much you loved those dependable events, whether it was Thanksgiving at Grandma's or a favorite bedtime story every night. It's worth the effort to establish a few God-honoring traditions. If you have kids of your own, they will likely carry them into their own families some day!

9. Lots of things bog us down—keeping a tidy house, overtime at work, planning meals, scheduling extracurricular activities, commuting, keeping up with the laundry, getting yard work done, all those little repairs the house needs. At the same time, our hearts are longing for time in God's Word, seasons of prayer, committing the Scriptures to memory, days of prayer and fasting, and a regular time for devotions with family and friends. How do we mesh all of these things together? It takes some gumption to set our houses in order. Sometimes, we must say no, even to "good" things for a time. Simplify your lifestyle enough to be sure the important things are covered. Then, you can prayerfully consider what more you can handle without losing sight of those basics.

Chapter 7

1. Prayer is one of the only ways that we are able to communicate with Almighty God. Some have compared it to other forms of communication: personal conversations, phone calls, letters. Others have compared it to the very air we breathe, essential for our spiritual life — we would suffocate without it. Are you drawing in deep breaths of rarified air, or is your prayer life limited to short gasps?

2. Prayer, in and of itself, is an admission that God is God. He is divine, greater, holier. We are human, imperfect, and needy. We turn to Him in submission, giving Him all the praise He deserves and pleading with Him to act on our behalf. Though we can come boldly before the throne of God (Heb. 4:16), we still acknowledge His authority over us. Prayer is also a way to bind our heart to His. By whispering to our Heavenly Father every thought and care, our spirits are drawn into His presence, and return with a sense of sweet assurance and peace.

3. Jesus knows after He returns to the Father, the disciples will be left alone, at the mercy of a world that will despise them. He prays the Father will keep His disciples safe — "keep them and care for them" (verse 11, NLT), protecting them from the Evil One (verse 15). Jesus wants for them to have unity (verse 11, NLT). And, He wants the Father to give them joy (verse 13).

4. "I pray for these followers, but I am also praying for all those who will believe in Me because of their teaching" (John 17:20, NCV). Hey! That's us! Jesus extended His prayer to those of us who, generations later, would believe.

5. "I will pray the Father, and He will give you another Helper, that He may abide with you forever" (John 14:16, NKJV). Jesus prayed that the Father would send the Holy Spirit, the Comforter, the Helper.

6. "Christ who died, and furthermore is also risen, who is even at the right hand of God, who also makes intercession for us" (Rom. 8:34, NKJV). "He is also able to save to the uttermost those who come to God through Him, since He always lives to make intercession for them" (Heb. 7:25, NKJV). This very moment, Jesus continues to pray on your behalf.

7. "Epaphras, who is one of you, a bondservant of Christ, greets you, always laboring fervently for you in prayers, that you may stand perfect and complete in all the will of God" (Col. 4:12, NKJV).

8. One wonderful way to enter into prayer is to pray the words of Scripture back to the God who inspired them. Find Bible prayers or other passages that speak to your heart, and then pray them for yourself, your family, your friends.

9. "The Spirit helps us with our weakness. We do not know how to pray as we should. But the Spirit Himself speaks to God for us, even begs God for us with deep feelings that words cannot explain" (Rom. 8:26, NCV). When we cannot find the words, the Spirit helps us to pray.

Chapter 8

1. "In everything give thanks; for this is the will of God in Christ Jesus for you" (1 Thess. 5:18, NKJV). Thankfulness!

2. We know that we are supposed to give thanks to God no matter what our circumstances might be. Sometimes, though, it's pretty hard to find a reason. After all, what's the point of some of the little annoyances that enter into our days? We have to just trust through it all, God is using these little trials to bring things to our attention, to allow us to act out our faith, and to eventually bring us forth as gold (1 Pet. 1:7)!

3. The Psalmist rehearses here the wonders of God's creation. God is the King over all gods, and all the earth belongs to Him.

4. "Don't worry about anything, but in all your prayers ask God for what you need, always asking him with a thankful heart" (Phil. 4:6, TEV). It seems as though we are to face the Lord with thankfulness, even when we are in need of something more! Even as we call upon His Name to come and rescue us, we can be bringing to mind those times when He has proven faithful.

5. "I will praise the name of God with a song, And will magnify Him with thanksgiving" (Ps. 69:30). "It is good to give thanks to the Lord, And to sing praises to Your name, O Most High" (Ps. 92:1). Whether you whistle it, hum it, or sing it out at the top of your lungs, a song of praise and thanksgiving is a wonderful way to say "thank you" to God!

6. Songs of thanks are many and varied. Some of the all-time favorites have been "Great is Thy Faithfulness," "Thank You Lord (for saving my soul)," "Give Thanks (with a grateful heart)." Even if the song doesn't exactly say "thank you," God sees the heart of praise and thanks that is offering up the song.

7. "For all things are for your sakes, that grace, having spread through the many, may cause thanksgiving to abound to the glory of God" (2 Cor. 4:15, NKJV). When thanksgiving abounds, God is glorified. When we live our lives with a grateful heart, God gets the glory.

8. "We give thanks to God always for you all, making mention of you in our prayers" (1 Thess. 1:2, NKJV). We should be thankful for each other, for fellow believers!

Chapter 9

1. Sanctification means holiness in the Scriptures, and to sanctify something is to make it holy.

2. Holy is usually defined as "set apart." In a way, holiness is hard to define. Only God is truly holy—it is one of His attributes, and sets Him apart from all else. Mostly, we associate the idea of "holy" with purity, perfection, sinlessness, and light. God is holy, and those He chooses are set apart for holiness as well. "You shall be holy to Me, for I the Lord am holy, and have separated you from the peoples, that you should be Mine" (Lev. 20:26, NKJV).

3. "He chose us in Him before the foundation of the world, that we should be holy and without blame before Him in love" (Eph. 1:4, NKJV). Even before Cain and Abel were a proverbial twinkle in Adam's eye, God knew who you would be, and He loved you, and He wanted you to be set apart for His glory.

4. "Be holy in all you do, just as God, the One who called you, is holy" (1 Pet. 1:15, NCV).

5. John 17:19, by the truth. 1 Thessalonians 5:23, by God Himself. Ephesians 5:26, by the Word (the Bible). Hebrews 10:10, by Jesus' sacrifice. 1 Timothy 4:5, by God's Word and by prayer. Numbers 15:40, by obedience to God. Romans 15:16, by the Holy Spirit. Hebrews 10:29, by Christ's blood.

6. "He will be a vessel for honor, sanctified and useful for the Master, prepared for every good work" (2 Tim. 2:21, NKJV). The New Living Translation calls us a "utensil God can use." We aren't saved to just sit and look pretty. God wants us to be useful to Him, so make yourself available for His plans!

7. We are "His own special people, zealous for good works" (Titus 2:14, NKJV). We are ready for good works! Zeal implies an excitement, eagerness, and a level of commitment that cannot be swayed from its purpose. Are you a willing vessel for the Lord, committed to His will for your life?

8. "Sanctify the Lord God in your hearts" (1 Pet. 3:15). We are taking an active stance here, by setting apart our hearts for God. Peter is encouraging us to commit ourselves to God's will, and make ourselves available to do whatever He wants.

Chapter 10

1. "God wants all people to eat and drink and be happy in their work, which are gifts from God" (Eccl. 3:13, NCV). Whatever your daily tasks may be, and whatever the food and drink that comes to your table, they are all gifts from God!

2. Though some of us might daydream about the chance to laze around with absolutely nothing to do, we would soon be bored. Work gives us a chance to exercise our creativity, stretch our minds, move our muscles, and use our gifts. Our tasks give us a sense of accomplishment, satisfaction, and pride. Honest work makes our rest sweeter, our food tastier, and our beds a taste of heaven at the end of a day!

3. If you are out to have "fun" in everything you do, life will quickly become very "not fun." If your tasks are inglorious, try to look at the bigger picture. There must be some way to redeem that time you spend on the job. Pray for God's transformation in your attitudes. Ask Him to show you a way to find satisfaction in completing your responsibilities.

4. Would a new computer, a new neighbor, a new microwave, a new car, a new coffee pot, or a new coat of paint really change that much? Don't wait for your list of grievances to be met before you are willing to move forward in God's will. He can use you right where you are, even if it isn't exactly where you want to be! The old adage is appropriate here: "Bloom where you're planted!"

5. The dictionary defines "contentment" as happiness with one's situation in life. Some would say that contentment is being satisfied with what you've got.

6. "Aspire to lead a quiet life, to mind your own business, and to work with your own hands" (1 Thess. 4:11, NKJV). Sounds like a pretty simple life to me!

7. Greed, envy, covetousness, jealousy, "the lust of the eyes"—You name it, we can be ensnared by it! Hebrews 13:5 says, "Let your conduct be without covetousness; be content with such things as you have. For He Himself has said, 'I will never leave you nor forsake you.'" Coveting breaks one of God's Ten Commandments! We don't need to look elsewhere for satisfaction, because according to this Hebrews passage, we have Jesus! Though our possessions on this earth may be fleeting, Jesus will never leave us.

8. "I have learned in whatever state I am, to be content" (Phil. 4:11, NKJV). Though Paul had many friends and followers, he could never be sure where God would send him. He traveled on foot and by boat. Sometimes he was welcomed, sometimes he was mocked and run out of town. He's been beaten, stoned, and shipwrecked. Yet Paul wrote these words from a prison cell!

9. "Now godliness with contentment is great gain" (1 Tim. 6:6, NKJV). The New Century Version puts it this way: "Serving God does make us very rich, if we are satisfied with what we have."

Chapter 11

1. Good food, good grades, good times, good news, the good old days, good deeds, good intentions, good Samaritans. Lots of the things in life that we enjoy or do can be called good. After all, when God created this world He made, He took one look and called it good.

2. "A good man out of the good treasure of his heart brings forth good things, and an evil man out of the evil treasure brings forth evil things" (Matt. 12:35, NKJV). Christians are able to do "good things" because of the transformation God has brought about in our hearts. We are now temples of the Holy Spirit. Instead of doing what comes naturally—acting selfishly or with ulterior motives—we are given the courage, the strength, and even a prompting to do the right thing.

3. It wouldn't be so bad if we could stay within our little group of Christian friends and just love and encourage one another until the good Lord returns. But Luke 6:33 says "Is that so wonderful? Even sinners do that much" (NLT). "I say to you, love your enemies, bless those who curse you, do good to those who hate you, and pray for those who spitefully use you and persecute you" (Matt. 5:44, NKJV). Jesus calls us to go against our better judgment. Who in their right mind loves the person who is out to get them? Yet our rivals, our competitors, our mockers—those we would instinctively draw away from—these are the ones we are called to shower with good.

4. There is a promise that if we are faithful in a small thing, we will be given greater things to manage. Also, every one of us longs to hear this welcome when we are finally called home. "Well done, good and faithful servant. Enter into the joy of your Lord" (Matt. 25:21, NKJV). Or, as my Dad would say, "Ya done good." Perhaps when we keep eternity in our view, and base our decisions on God's opinions, we will find it easier to choose the good.

5. "This is the will of God, that by doing good you may put to silence the ignorance of foolish men" (1 Pet. 2:15, NKJV). The integrity of our lives should be such that no one can make any accusations against us. When foolish people try to point fingers at you, it will be obvious to all who know your lives their charges are baseless.

6. "What credit is it if, when you are beaten for your faults, you take it patiently? But when you do good and suffer, if you take it patiently, this is commendable before God" (1 Pet. 2:20, NKJV). There's no glory in getting what you deserve. Maintain your integrity in the face of scrutiny, and don't be tempted to prove yourself. God asks us to take such persecution with patience and grace. That is hard to do, but commendable in God's eyes.

7. "Let your light so shine before men, that they may see your good works and glorify your Father in heaven" (Matt. 5:16, NKJV). Our good works glorify God, and they also point others in His direction. We are like Christian billboards!

8. Submission to our husbands, godly behavior, inner beauty, a gentle and quiet spirit, trusting God—all these things are said to make us daughters of Sarah, and truly beautiful.

Chapter 12

1. Those closest to us can be family and friends, but don't forget that your circle of support includes those who pray for you and those who you pray for. All of us who are believers are knit together somehow.

2. God has assured us that though His way will prove the best way in the end, the path is not an easy one. The life of a Christian will include trials, temptations, pitfalls, and persecution. We must apply ourselves, build our relationship with our Savior, and encourage one another along the way if we wish to "receive the promise" at the end.

3. Prayers, kind words, wise counsel, shared laughter, a shoulder to cry on, moral support in difficult decisions, a note of encouragement, a quick hug, a nod of support, a wink. Those whose lives become entwined with our own can help build each other up, and make the difficulties of life more bearable.

4. Those who have no endurance end up stumbling at the first sign of trouble. They have not rooted themselves in God, and have nothing to draw from when life gets hard. Without a source of strength, they are doomed before they even begin.

5. Paul was willing to endure every kind of trial and persecution here on earth because of fellow believers. He wanted more men and women to be reached through his preaching. For the sake of each soul that God would touch, he would hang in there. On the other hand, Paul was looking forward to heaven, for he says "if we endure, we shall also reign with Him" (2 Tim. 2:12, NKJV). He knew that Jesus would reward his obedience in the end.

6. "I do not claim that I have already succeeded or have already become perfect. I keep striving to win the prize for which Christ Jesus has already won me to himself" (Phil. 3:12, TEV). None of us will reach perfection on this side of heaven. Paul struggled with the same kinds of things we all do. Christ is at work in each of us, bringing us closer and closer to what He wants us to be. None of us will "arrive" until we actually arrive in glory!

7. What a beautiful statement: "We count them blessed who endure" (James 5:11, NKJV). Doesn't that just make you want to hang in there one more day? one more hour? at least for the next few minutes?

8. When a few people are left with the weight of responsibility on their shoulders, it does not take long for them to grow weary under the burden. Even good things, like work within the church, can drag down a Christian who is not being supported by their fellow believers. This is when it is so important to run the race together, making sure that a hand is ready to reach out to anyone who needs a little lift.

9. Galatians 6 says "And let us not grow weary while doing good, for in due season we shall reap if we do not lose heart." Paul says "Hang in there!" "Don't give up!" It will all be worth it in the end.

✦ Acknowledgments ✦

© Clairmont, Patsy; Johnson, Barbara; Meberg, Marilyn; and Swindoll, Luci, *Joy Breaks*, (Grand Rapids: Zondervan Publishing House, 1997)

© Clairmont, Patsy; Johnson, Barbara; Meberg, Marilyn; and Swindoll, Luci, *The Joyful Journey*, (Grand Rapids: Zondervan Publishing House, 1998)

© Clairmont, Patsy, *The Best Devotions of Patsy Clairmont*, (Grand Rapids: Zondervan Publishing House, 2001)

© Johnson, Barbara, *The Best Devotions of Barbara Johnson*, (Grand Rapids: Zondervan Publishing House, 2001)

© Meberg, Marilyn, *The Best Devotions of Marilyn Meberg*, (Grand Rapids: Zondervan Publishing House, 2001)

© Swindoll, Luci, *The Best Devotions of Luci Swindoll*, (Grand Rapids: Zondervan Publishing House, 2001)

© Walsh, Sheila, *The Best Devotions of Sheila Walsh*, (Grand Rapids: Zondervan Publishing House, 2001)

© Wells, Thelma, *The Best Devotions of Thelma Wells*, (Grand Rapids: Zondervan Publishing House, 2001)

© Women of Faith, Inc., *We Brake for Joy*, (Grand Rapids: Zondervan Publishing House, 1997)

ADDITIONAL
RESOURCES

✦ WHAT SHALL WE STUDY NEXT? ✦

**Women of Faith has three other study guides out right now
that will draw you closer to God.**

Living Above Worry and Stress

Consider the lilies, how they grow: they neither toil nor spin; and yet I say to you, even Solomon in all his glory was not arrayed like one of these. If then God so clothes the grass, which today is in the field and tomorrow is thrown into the oven, how much more will He clothe you, O you of little faith?

Luke 12:27-28, NKJV

The words echo back to us from years gone by. We first learned it in a Vacation Bible School one summer or from a dear Sunday school teacher—the voice of Jesus calling us to consider the lilies. The lesson was a simple one: don't worry. If God would give the flowers such pretty petals, dressing them more grandly than wealthy King Solomon could manage, He will provide for our needs too.

Unfortunately, the call to consider the lilies is left on a dusty shelf somewhere. It's probably right next to the old plea to stop and smell the roses. We're too busy for stopping. We're too rushed for consideration. Our "to do" lists are long. Our day timers are booked. Our time is money. We can't keep up.

We are busy people. We have responsibilities at work. We have responsibilities at home. We have responsibilities at church. We have responsibilities at school. We have responsibilities within our communities. We care for the needs of our parents, our husbands, our children, our siblings, our employers, our closest friends. Most days, it is more than we can handle. Our hearts are overwhelmed. We are stressed out. We are worried. We dread tomorrow.

In the midst of all this everyday turmoil, our hearts long for a place of peace. We know God has promised us rest. We know He says we don't have to worry about tomorrow. He promised to calm our fears. Yet we barely have time to whisper a prayer, let alone study our Bibles. If you have been struggling, come. Let's take a little time to explore the Scriptures, and find some practical guidelines for laying aside our fears, our worry, and even our stress. You really can discover a place of peace.

Living in Jesus

Those who become Christians become new persons. They are not the same any-more, for the old life is gone. A new life has begun!

2 Corinthians 5:17, NLT

Have you ever read books just to escape the never-ending dull-ness of everyday life? Through the chapters of some paperback, we experience the shadows of an existence that seems more interesting, more exciting, more appealing than what our own day has to offer. Damsels find unfailing love, sleuths seek out elusive clues, strangers form unlikely alliances, adventurers cross unfamiliar terrains, and they all live happily ever after. In comparison, we feel boring, listless, and wistful.

Little do we realize that as believers, we have been ushered into a life that rivals the plot of any mere story! We have become leading ladies in a thrilling tale of epic proportions. There's something for everyone: combat, romance, intrigue, drama, rescue, duplicity, charac-ter development, action, adventure, complex subplots, moral dilemmas, sacrifice, tear jerking, subtle humor, slapstick, subterfuge, betrayal, showdowns, discovery, unexpected twists, irony, paradise, and a happy ending.

The Christian life is vibrant, mysterious, and beautiful. In a word—sensational! Open your eyes to the wonder of a life knit with the divine. Jesus has called you, chosen you, changed you. Your life is caught up with His, transformed into something altogether new. Jesus is your intimate friend—familiar, inseparable, precious. He has called you His beloved, and made you fantastic promises. Your life is a never-ending story that will continue to unfold throughout eternity.

All because of what you are *in Him.*

Adventurous Prayer: Talking with God

Prayer is reaching out to touch Someone — namely, your Creator. In the process He touches you.

Barbara Johnson

What's the big deal about prayer? We know we should all do it more often, take it more seriously, and give it more time — but we don't. Does that mean that prayer is optional? After all, some of the other spiritual disciplines seem pretty outdated, like fasting and solitude. Who has time for that? That kind of stuff is for monks, nuns, and pastors. We've gotten along okay without it.

So, does prayer fit into the *non*-essentials of the Christian walk? Prayer must be that "in case of emergency" last-resort kind of spiritual tool. Right?

Shame on you!

Prayer isn't some kind of requirement for believers. It is a privilege! You have the ear of the Divine. Prayer is our path to the adventure of building a relationship with our Savior.

God knows what's going on in your life. The Creator of all that is stoops to hear the lisping of toddlers. The Sustainer of every living thing hears the groans and sighs of the aging. He is aware of every thought, every choice, every move you make — but He is waiting for you to turn to Him and tell Him about it.

God listens to you. He will answer you.

The Complete Women of Faith™ Study Guide Series Available Now

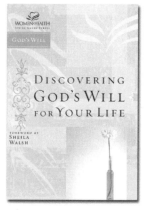

Discovering God's
Will for Your Life
0-7852-4983-4

Living Above
Worry and Stress
0-7852-4986-9

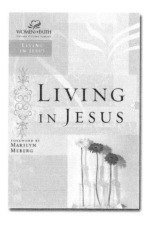

Living in Jesus
0-7852-4985-0

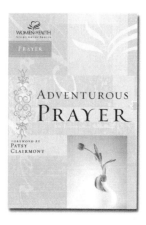

Adventurous Prayer
0-7852-4984-2

WHO DO YOU HAVE IN MIND?

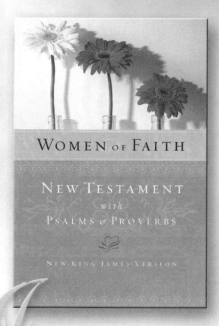

OTHER PRODUCTS BY WOMEN OF FAITH™

Available at fine bookstores everywhere.